FOUNDATIONS OF COLOR

FOUNDATIONS OF COLOR

JEFF DAVIS

TEMPE DIGITAL

█ TEMPE DIGITAL

7650 South McClintock Drive
Suite 103-292
Tempe, AZ 85284

First edition © 2015 Tempe Digital LLC

All rights reserved.

Except for quotations used in articles, reviews, and book listings, no part of this book may be reproduced, distributed, or transmitted in any form or by any means, including photocopying, recording, or other electronic or mechanical methods, without the prior written permission of Tempe Digital LLC.

Text, illustrations, and design: Jeff Davis

Cover image: Jeff Davis, **color palette 13**, 2011, digital c-print (single edition), 40 x 40 in. © *Jeff Davis*

Library of Congress Control Number: 2015902147

ISBN-13: 978-0-9861637-0-8
ISBN-10: 0-9861637-0-8

For product information, please email info@tempedigital.com

CONTENTS

PREFACE

Foundations of Color is a straightforward investigation of the basic principles of color theory. It introduces the defining properties of color, presents systems for organizing and relating colors, and examines how colors interact towards varying compositional effects. As a follow-up to *Foundations of Design*, this text has been written to be accessible by anyone with an interest in art or design. *Foundations of Color* strives to provide a conceptual framework for exploring and understanding the vast world of color.

ACKNOWLEDGMENTS

I would like to sincerely thank everyone who helped make this book possible.

To Cory Arcangel, Jesse Chapman, Vince Contarino, Petra Cortright, Gabriele Evertz, Kim Fisher, Matt Fontaine, Claudia Hart, Ridley Howard, Dion Johnson, Jessica Labatte, Luisa Lambri, Rafael Lozano-Hemmer, Matt Mignanelli, Yunhee Min, Takeshi Murata, Frank Nitsche, Amy Park, Ester Partegàs, Jon Pestoni, Zak Prekop, Casey Reas, Boo Ritson, Jason Salavon, Ali Smith, Robert Swain, Tony Tasset, Ben Weiner, Patrick Wilson, and Jonas Wood for your creativity and consideration.

To Professor Rupprecht for teaching me the Albers way.

To my parents for the freedom and encouragement to pursue my dreams.

To Rob and Ryan for your endless curiosity and inspiration.

And to Kelly, once again, for your unwavering love and support.

ABOUT THE AUTHOR

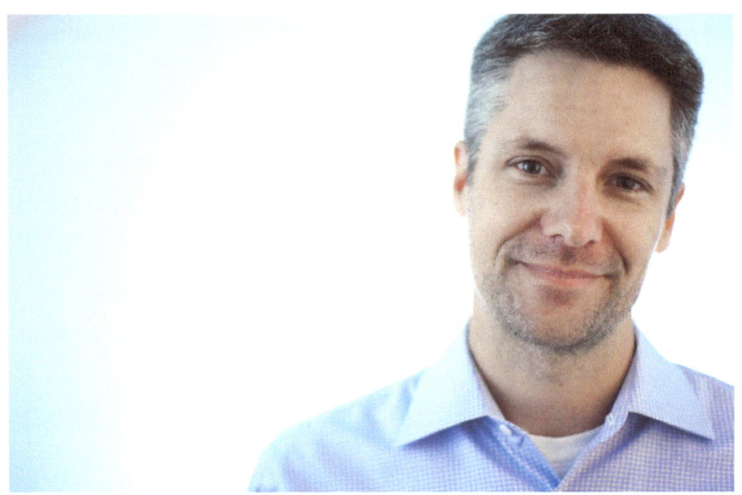

Jeff Davis currently serves as program director for the Art Foundations department at the Art Institute of Pittsburgh—Online Division, where he leads faculty and curriculum development. Prior to his role as program director, Jeff served as a faculty member teaching courses in design fundamentals and color theory. He is also the author of *Foundations of Design*, an introductory textbook for art and design students.

Jeff is a practicing digital artist and has exhibited his work throughout the United States. He received his BA degree in Mathematics and Studio Art from Lawrence University and his MFA degree in Painting and Drawing from the School of the Art Institute of Chicago. He currently lives in Tempe, Arizona with his wife and two children.

For more information, please visit: http://www.jeffgdavis.com

1

1   COLOR

Color is one of the most powerful visual forces in nature. Color identifies and characterizes. Color deceives. It attracts and repels, stimulates and calms. Color differentiates and color unifies. The artist and educator Johannes Itten wrote, "Each individual color is a universe in itself."* This statement conveys the vast complexity of color and the depth of its possible exploration. The study of color is a lifelong endeavor, and anyone working in art or design should strive to become a conscious observer of color in his or her surroundings. This supports a deeper understanding of how colors are defined and organized, how colors relate and interact, and how color can influence a composition.

The first step toward understanding color is learning how we see color. Our perception of color is a visual experience that

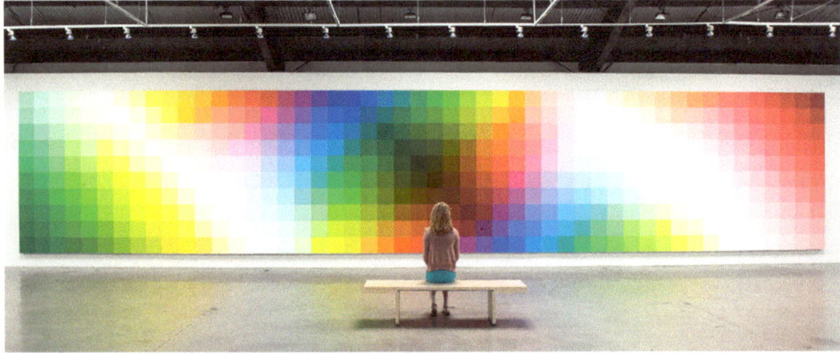

COLOR. Robert Swain, **Untitled, 10 x 50**, 2014. Acrylic on birch panels, 10 x 50 feet. © *Robert Swain. Photography by Yao Zu Lu. Courtesy of the artist.*

* Johannes Itten, *The Elements of Color*, trans. Ernst Van Hagen. (New York: John Wiley & Sons, 1970)..

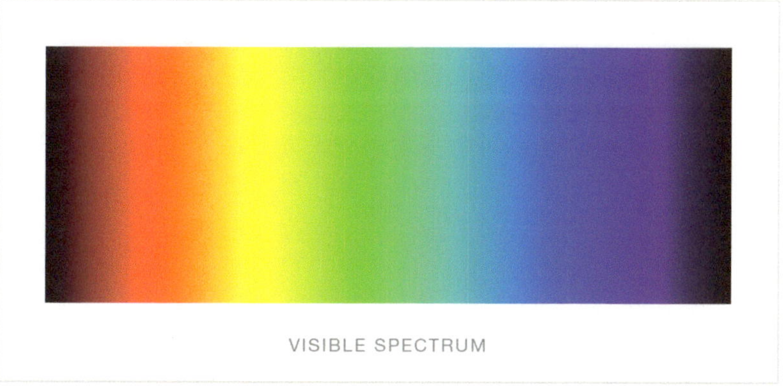

VISIBLE SPECTRUM

Figure 1-1

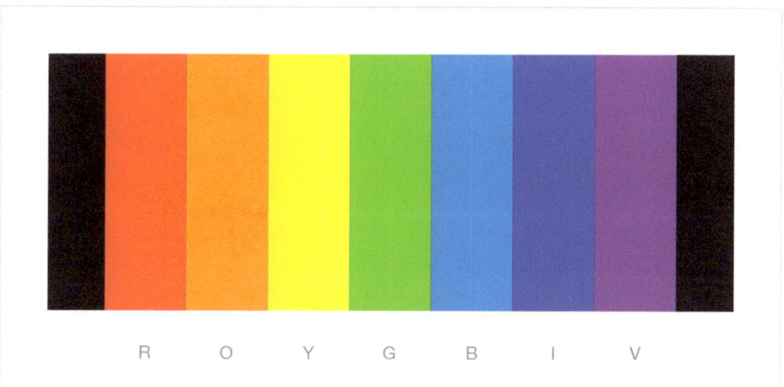

Figure 1-2

begins with light. **Light** is a form of electromagnetic radiation that can be recognized by the human eye. The electromagnetic wavelengths we are able to see form the **visible spectrum**, with individual wavelengths of light corresponding to distinct hues of color (1-1). These are the hues of the rainbow, commonly abbreviated as **ROYGBIV** for red, orange, yellow, green, blue, indigo, and violet (1-2). Combining red and violet, the two hues at opposite ends of the spectrum, produces additional hues in

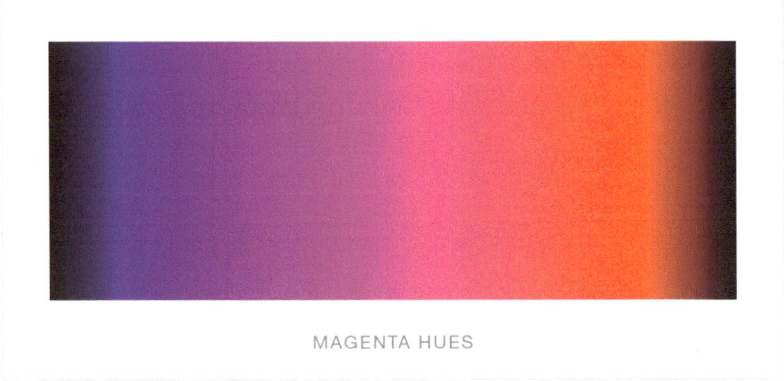

MAGENTA HUES

Figure 1-3

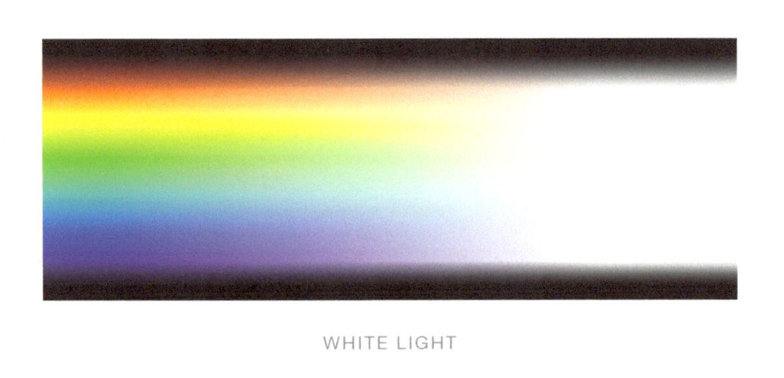

WHITE LIGHT

Figure 1-4

the magenta range that are outside of the visible spectrum (1-3). Combining all hues in the visible spectrum produces white light (1-4).

What we perceive as color however is not a physical property of light. Individual wavelengths of light are not themselves colored. Instead, our perception of color is a physiological response to a light stimulus. When certain wavelengths of light reach our eyes, our brain interprets that stimulus as color. In

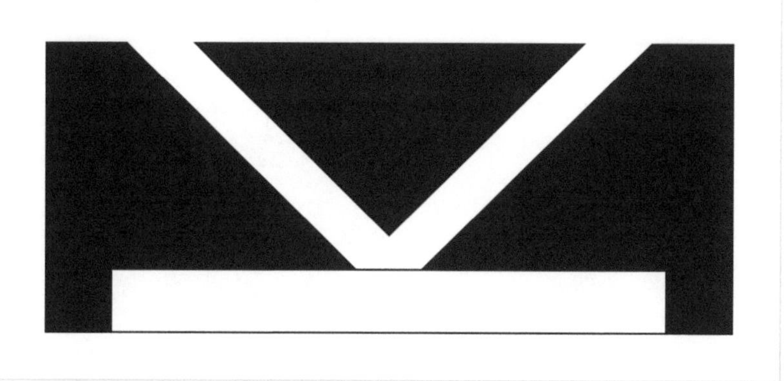

Figure 1-5

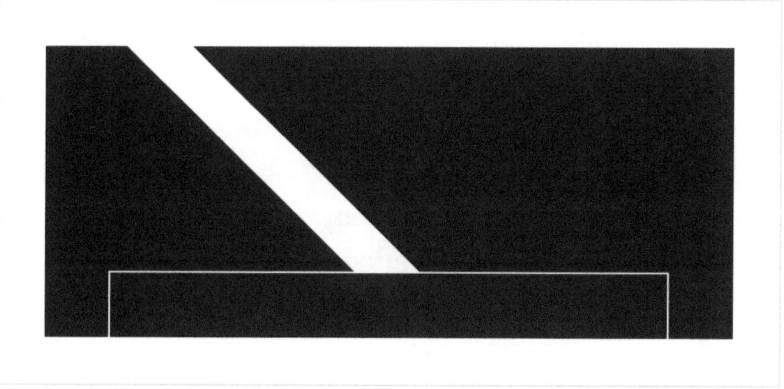

Figure 1-6

most cases, light reaches our eyes indirectly. When white light strikes a colored surface, certain wavelengths are reflected and others are absorbed. Those that are reflected determine the color of the object. Objects that are white reflect nearly all wavelengths of light (1-5). Objects that are black absorb nearly all wavelengths of light (1-6). Objects with other colors selectively reflect wavelengths of light that correspond to their color and absorb all other wavelengths. For example, a red object reflects the wavelengths that correspond to the hue

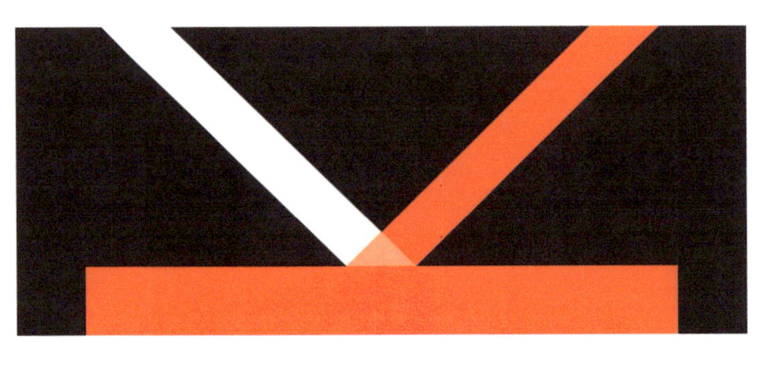

Figure 1-7

of red and absorbs any remaining wavelengths (1-7). Light can also reach our eyes directly without being reflected off a colored surface. For example, televisions and computer monitors project wavelengths of light directly to our eyes, which we then perceive as color. Whether light reaches our eyes directly or indirectly, it is the combination of wavelengths that determines the color we perceive.

An individual's response to color is a unique experience based on a number of factors. Associations from the natural world, cultural traditions, and fashion trends blend with personal experience and preference to shape our experience of color. Color communicates on many different levels. Intellectually, color conveys information and ideas. It identifies, distinguishes, and has symbolic meaning. Emotionally, color expresses feeling and creates mood. It can recall strong memories and associations. Physiologically, color directly affects our behavior. It can excite and stimulate, or calm and soothe. Our interpretation of color is a complex and multifaceted experience.

2

2   HUE

Every **color** in existence is defined by the properties of hue, value, and saturation. Individual colors can be pinpointed through the unique combination of these three properties. Each defining property is independent from one another and their combination yields a specific color.

Hue is the first defining property of color. It is the name of a color in its purest state. When we describe a color as red, orange, yellow, green, blue, or violet, we are referring to the hue of that color (2-1). These basic terms can be combined to create intermediate descriptions such as red-orange or blue-violet.

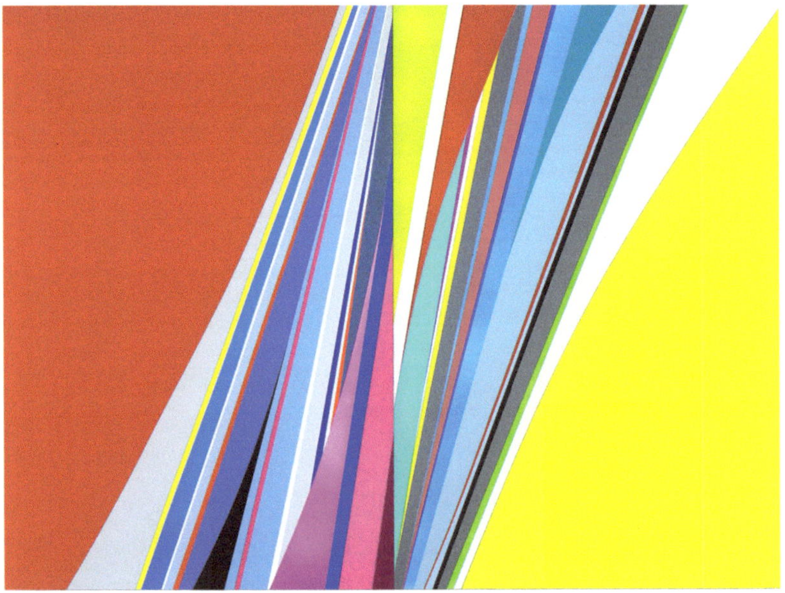

VARIATION IN HUE. Dion Johnson, **Twist**, 2013. Acrylic on canvas, 60 x 80 inches. © Dion Johnson. Courtesy of the artist and Western Project, Los Angeles.

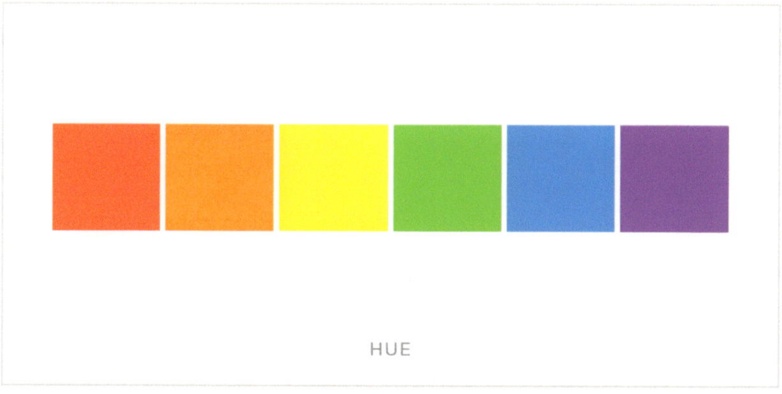

Figure 2-1

The concept of hue is often confused with the broader concept of color, with the terms being used incorrectly as synonyms. Hue is a single property of color, while color is a combination of three different properties. For example, pink and maroon both share the hue of red but are unique colors due to differences in value and saturation.

While our response to color is personal and shaped by past experience, each hue also has innate characteristics based on its appearance in the natural world and its association with cultural conventions. Red is stimulating, the color of blood and intense heat. Red symbolizes both love and anger. Orange is the color of the sun, energetic and cheerful. Orange also denotes warning and danger. Yellow is bright, the color of daylight and gold. Yellow symbolizes both hope and fear. Green is the color of nature, signifying growth and renewal. Green is also associated with envy, jealousy, and sickness. Blue is peaceful, the color of the sky and the ocean. Blue also expresses cold and sadness. Violet is rare in nature and mysterious. Violet is the color of luxury and royalty.

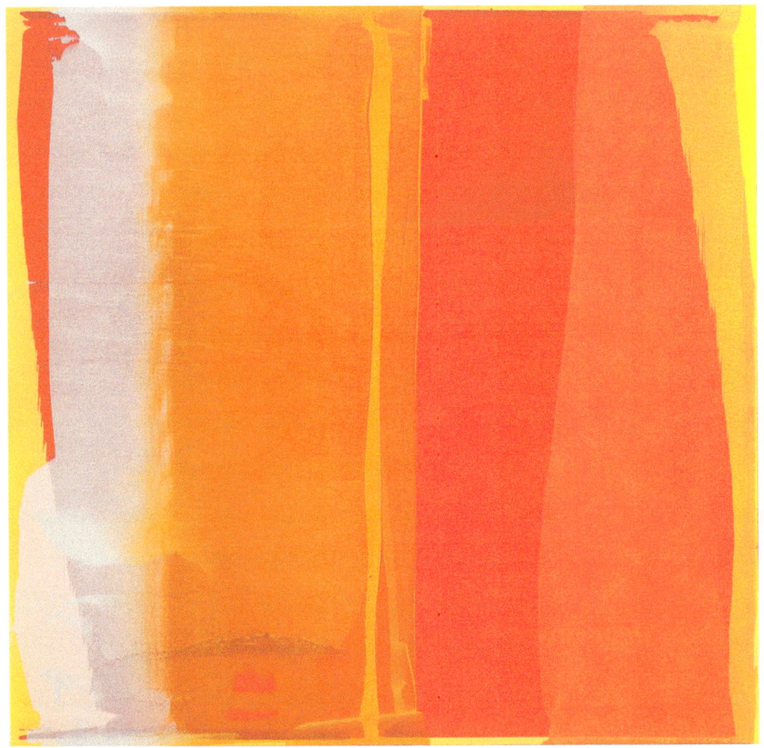

WARM HUES. Yunhee Min, **Into the Sun #5**, 2013. Acrylic on canvas, 60 x 60 inches. © Yunhee Min. Photography by Robert Wedemeyer. Courtesy of the artist and Susanne Vielmetter Los Angeles Projects.

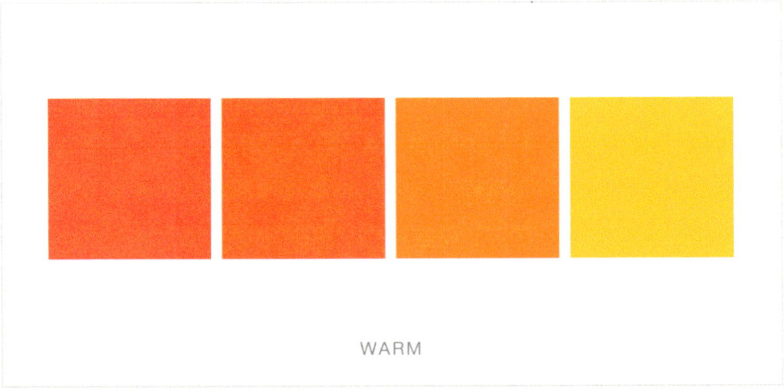

Figure 2-2

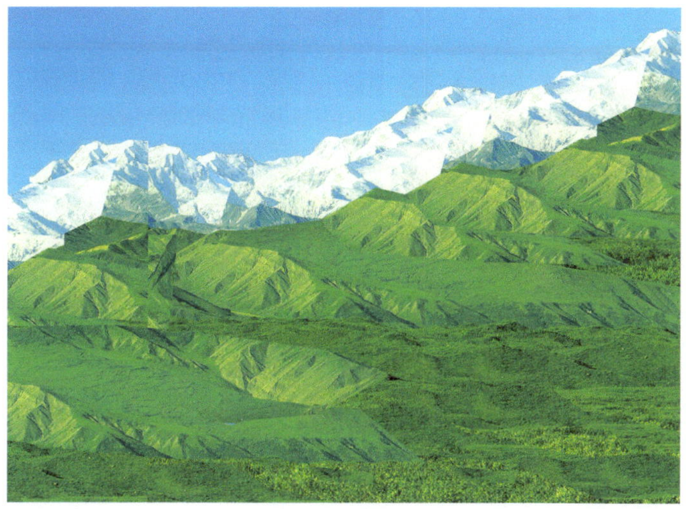

COOL HUES. Petra Cortright, **Cold Landscape**, 2005. JPEG image, 1600 x 1200 px. © *Petra Cortright. Courtesy of the artist.*

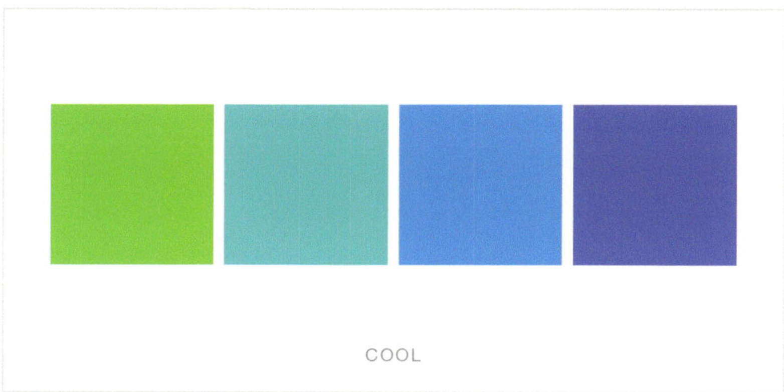

Figure 2-3

Another way to describe hue is through temperature. Hues such as red, orange, and yellow are associated with sunlight and fire and considered **warm** (2-2). Hues such as green and blue are associated with foliage, water, and snow and considered **cool** (2-3). Warm hues are generally more active and aggressive, while cool hues tend to be passive and calm.

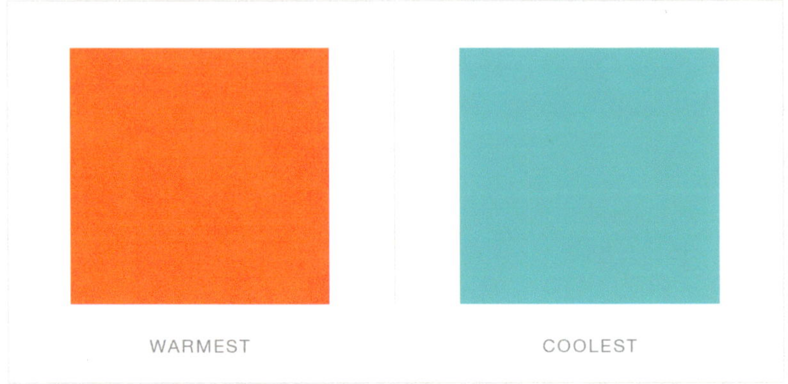

Figure 2-4

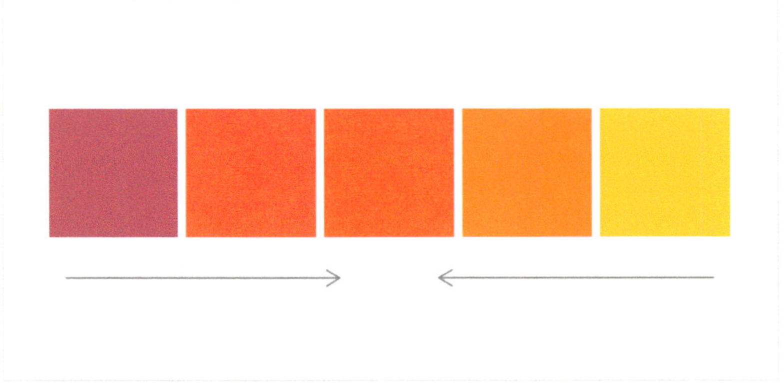

Figure 2-5

It is common to classify red-orange as the warmest hue and blue-green as the coolest hue (2-4). As a hue increases in similarity to red-orange, it becomes warmer in temperature (2-5). As a hue increases in similarity to blue-green, it becomes cooler in temperature (2-6). The temperature of a hue can also be ambiguous with no tendency towards warm or cool. Yellow-green and violet are good examples of hues with ambiguous temperatures (2-7). In addition, the perceived

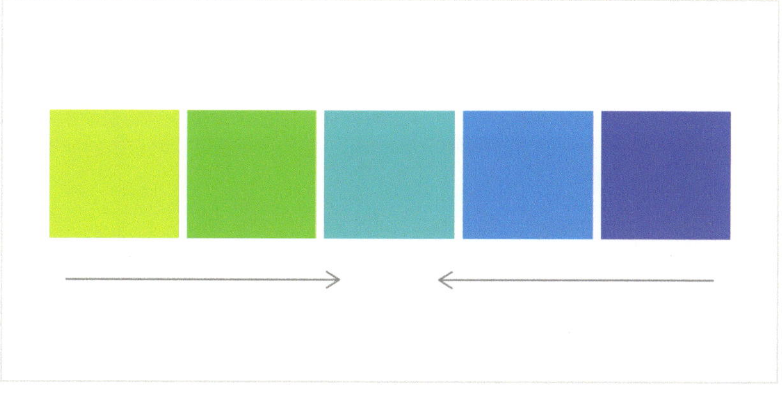

Figure 2-6

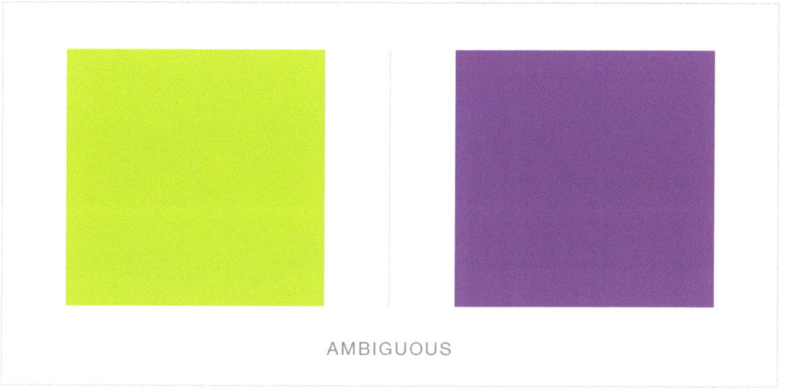

Figure 2-7

temperature of a hue is a relative experience. The same hue may appear cooler when compared to a warm hue, and warmer when compared to a cool hue.

VALUE

3

3 VALUE

The second defining property of color is value. **Value** is the relative lightness or darkness of a color (3-1). When we describe a color as being light or dark, we are referring to the value of that color. The specific value of a color is determined by the quantity of light it reflects or projects. Because we tend to have

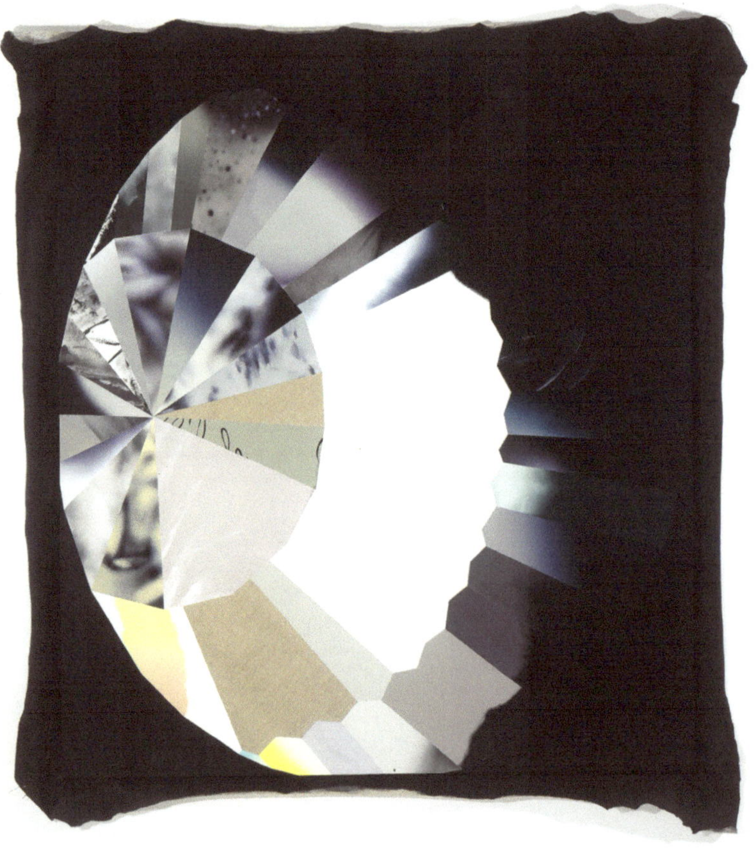

VARIATION IN VALUE. Kim Fisher, **Last Quarter**, 2008. Oil on linen, 72 x 63 inches. © Kim Fisher. Courtesy of the artist; Shane Campbell Gallery, Chicago; Modern Institute, Glasgow; and China Art Objects, Los Angeles.

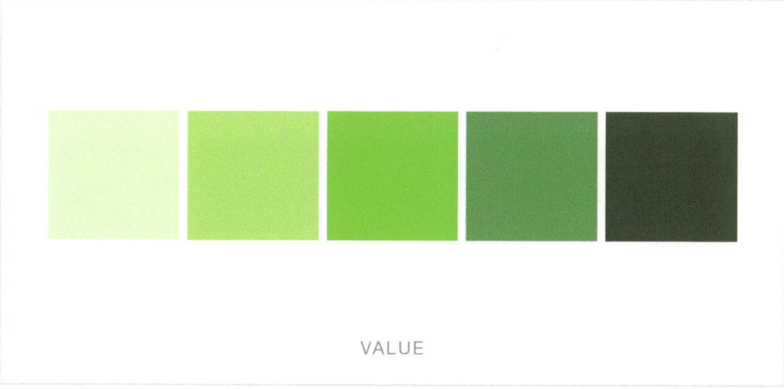

Figure 3-1

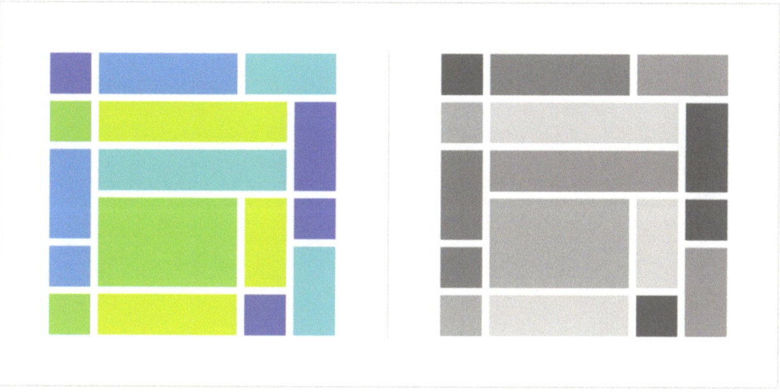

Figure 3-2

a stronger response to a color's hue or saturation, sometimes it can be difficult to distinguish the value of a color. Taking a black and white photograph or digitally converting an image to grayscale eliminates the properties of hue and saturation and translates colors into values of gray (3-2).

The value of an individual color can be measured through the use of a **value scale**. At one end of the value scale sits white, the lightest possible value, and at the opposite end is

LIGHT VALUES. Luisa Lambri, **Untitled (Strathmore Apartments, #05A)**, 2002. Laserchrome print, 43 ¼ x 51 ⅛ inches. © *Luisa Lambri. Courtesy of the artist and Luhring Augustine, New York.*

black, the darkest possible value. These two endpoints are connected by a sequence of intermediate grays, ordered from light to dark. While this sequence of grays could be rendered as a continuous range of value, value scales are normally constructed to have a distinct number of steps, each representing an even transition in value (3-3). An individual color can then be compared to each step in the scale to determine its closest value.

Colors with value levels near white on the value scale are considered light. Light values tend to be airy and soft. Colors with value levels near the middle of the value scale have intermediate values. Intermediate values are more relaxed

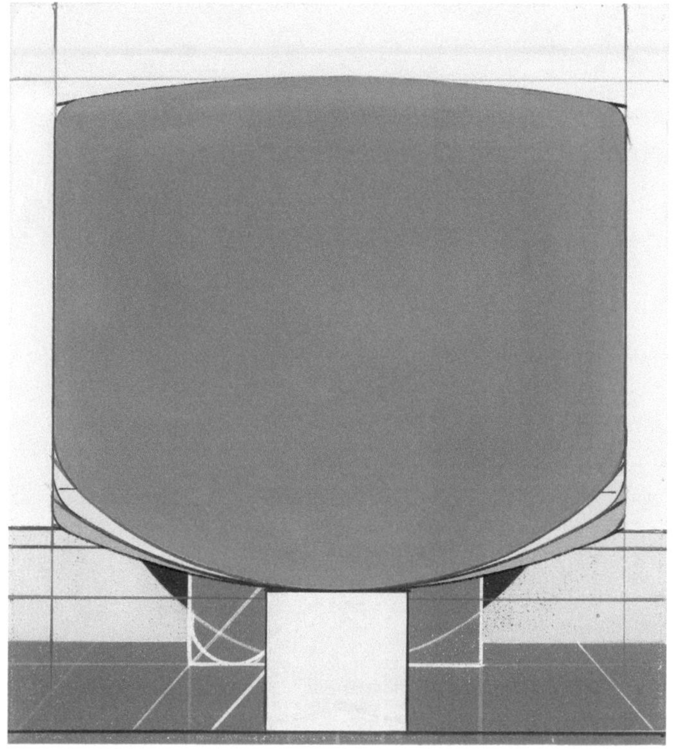

INTERMEDIATE VALUES. Frank Nitsche, **PAP-31**, 2013. Oil on canvas, 16.1 x 14.1 inches. © *Frank Nitsche. Photography by Thomas Mueller. Courtesy of the artist and Koenig & Clinton, New York.*

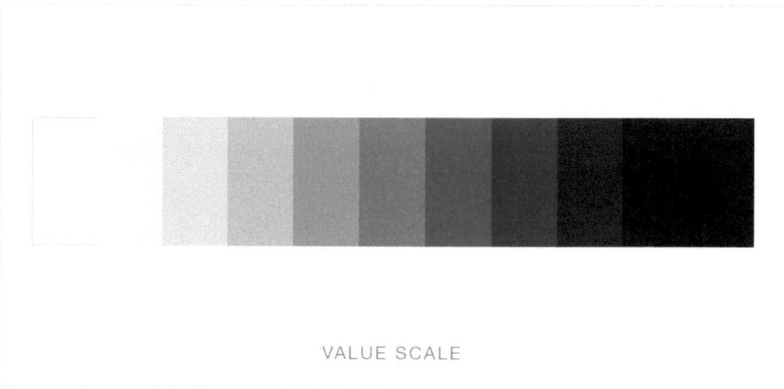

Figure 3-3

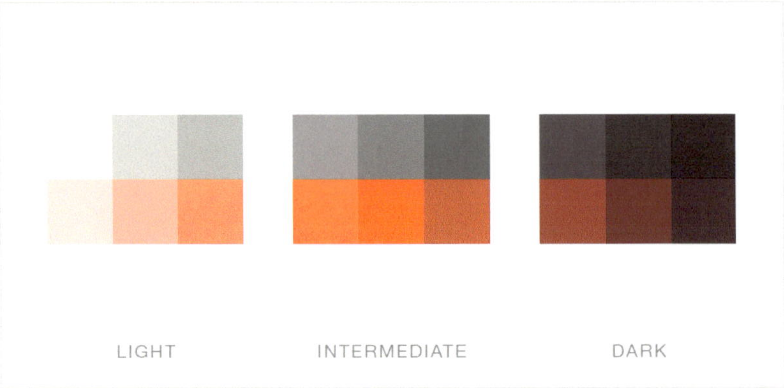

Figure 3-4

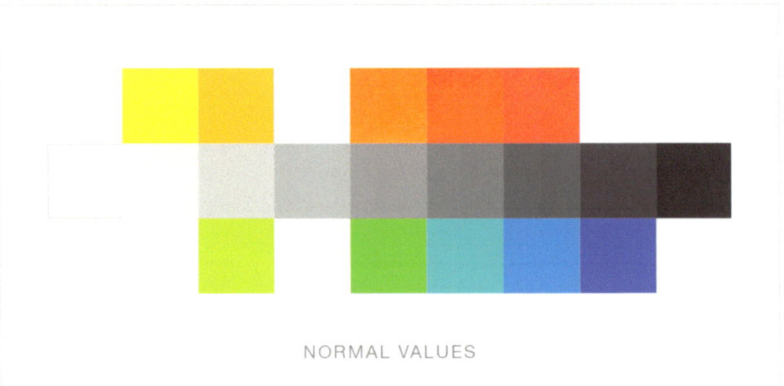

Figure 3-5

and solid. Colors with value levels near black on the value scale are considered dark. Dark values tend to be heavy and subdued (3-4).

A specific use for a value scale is determining the normal value of a hue. The **normal value** of a hue is its inherent value when at maximum saturation. For example, pure yellow has a light normal value while blue-violet has a dark normal value. Other hues have normal values between these two extremes (3-5).

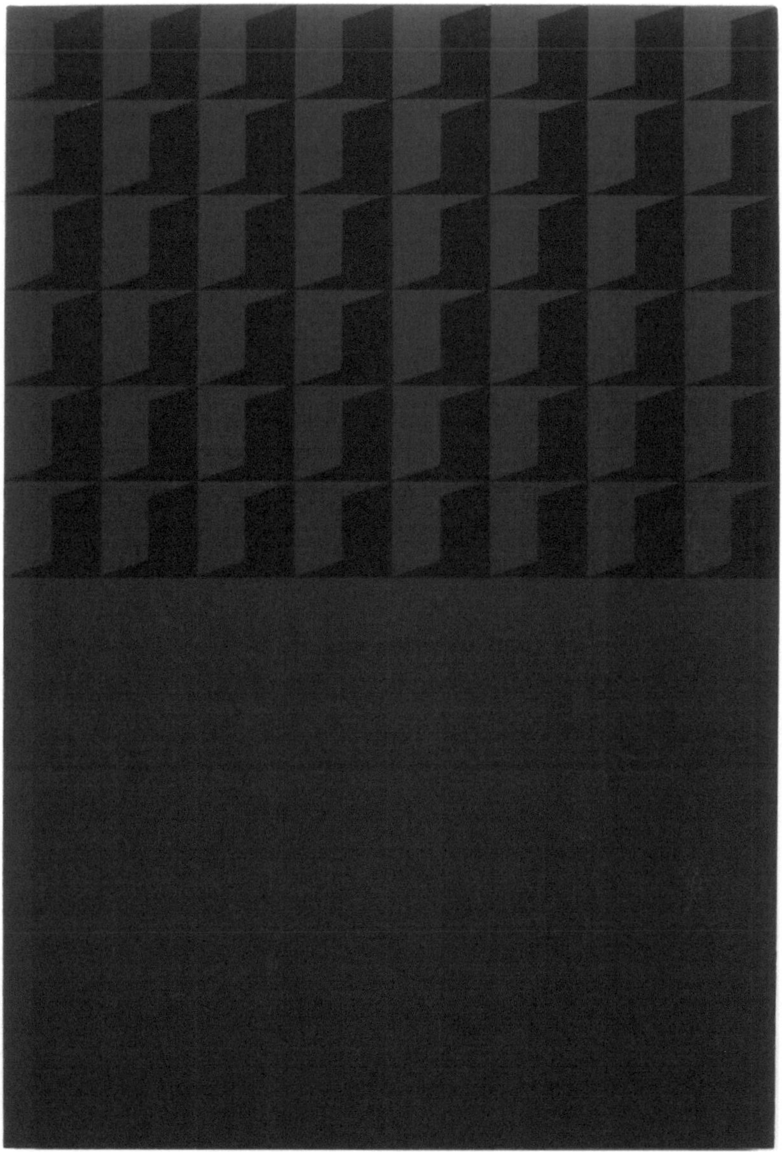

DARK VALUES. Matt Mignanelli, **Siege**, 2013. Gloss and matte enamel on canvas, 36 x 24 inches. © *Matt Mignanelli. Courtesy of the artist.*

SATURATION

4

4   SATURATION

The final defining property of color is saturation. Also known as **intensity** or **chroma, saturation** is the relative strength or purity of a color (4-1). Colors with high saturation are described as bright, strong, or pure. Colors with low saturation are described as dull, weak, or diluted.

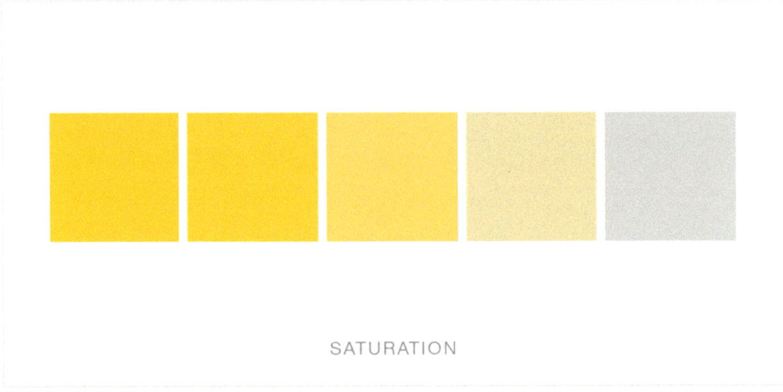

Figure 4-1

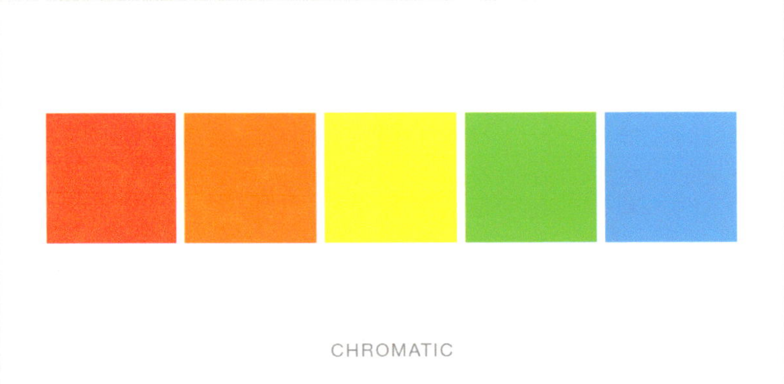

Figure 4-2

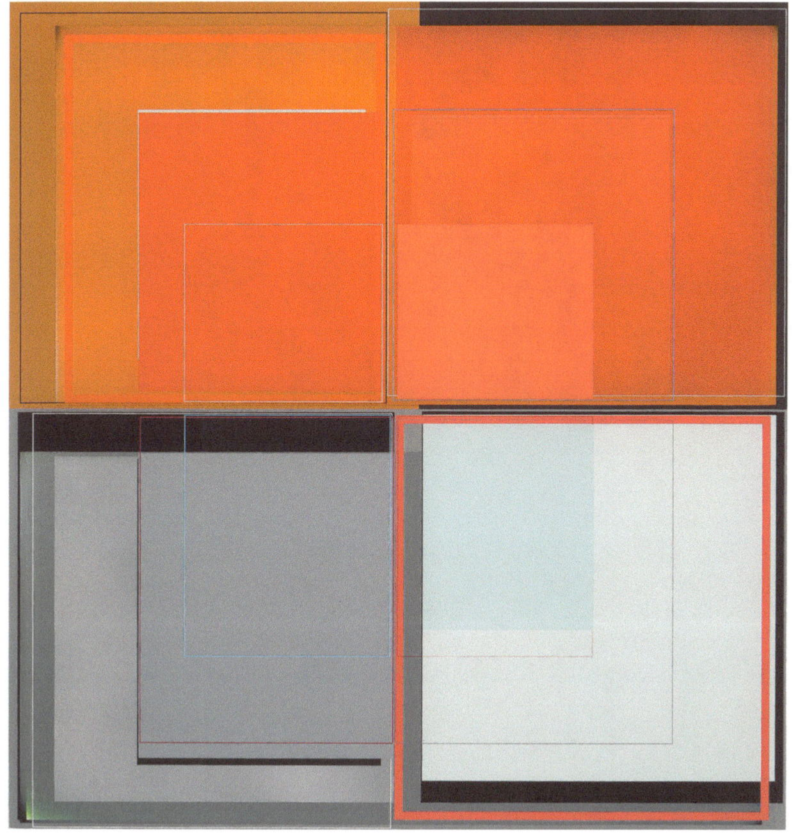

VARIATION IN SATURATION. Patrick Wilson, **Hot Wings**, 2013. Acrylic on canvas, 72 x 67 inches. © *Patrick Wilson. Photography by Robert Wedemeyer. Courtesy of the artist and Susanne Vielmetter Los Angeles Projects.*

Chromatic colors have a noticeable level of saturation, allowing their hue quality to be perceptible (4-2). Colors at full saturation have maximum intensity and are the most vivid. These are the colors of the visible spectrum and do not contain white, black, or gray. Fully saturated colors are dynamic and loud. Colors

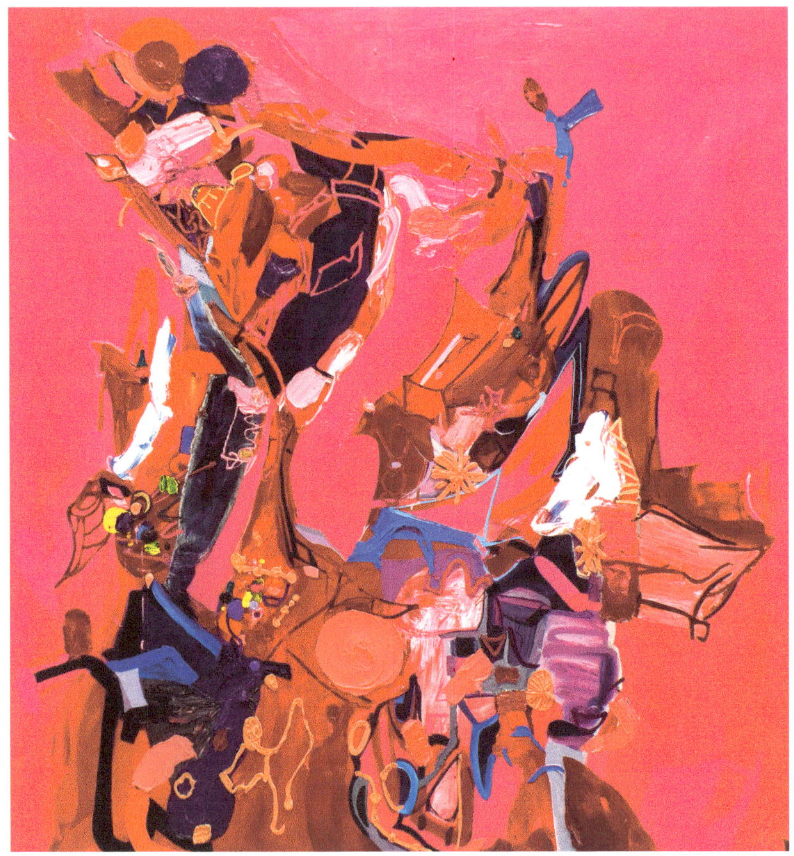

CHROMATIC COLORS. Ali Smith, **Geek Love**, 2008. Oil and acrylic on canvas, 92 x 84 inches. © *Ali Smith / Mark Moore Gallery. Courtesy of the artist and Mark Moore Gallery.*

with a moderate degree of saturation are also chromatic, but contain a small proportion of white, black, or gray. Colors with moderate saturation are less assertive than colors at full saturation. **Neutral** colors have a low level of saturation, making their hue quality less distinguishable (4-3). They are muted and contain a large proportion of white, black, or gray. Neutral colors are relaxed, somber, and quiet. **Achromatic**

NEUTRAL COLORS. Jason Salavon, **Portrait (Hals)**, 2009. Digital c-print, 40 x 30 inches. © *Jason Salavon. Courtesy of the artist and Mark Moore Gallery.*

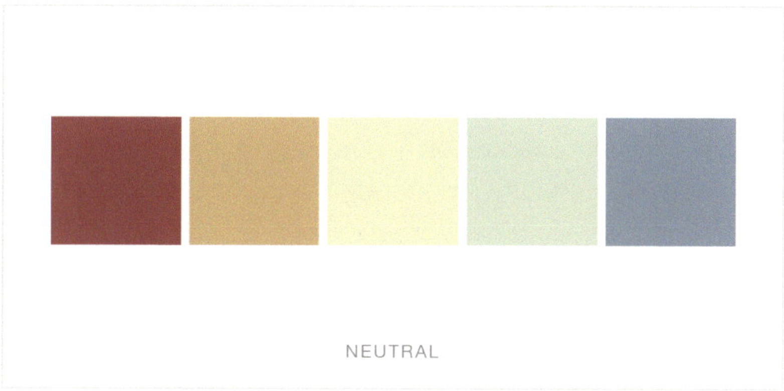

Figure 4-3

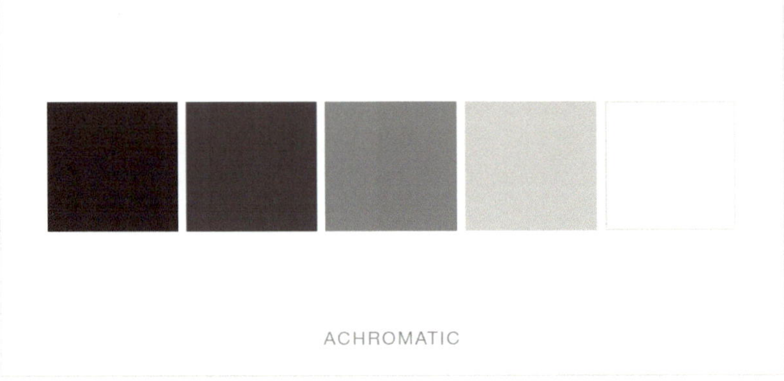

Figure 4-4

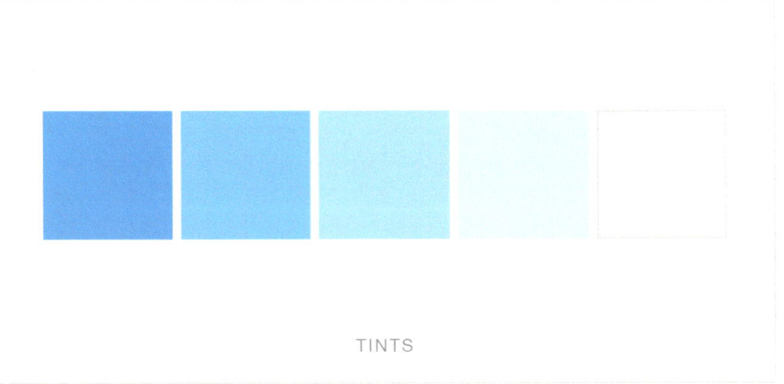

Figure 4-5

colors are without saturation and have no discernible hue (4-4). Black, white, and fully desaturated grays are all achromatic. Achromatic colors convey stability and sophistication.

Given a fixed hue, a wide range of color variations called tints, shades, and tones can be achieved through the addition of white, black, or gray. When adding an achromatic color to a pure hue, the saturation of the resulting color always decreases while the hue remains the same. This is because the purity of

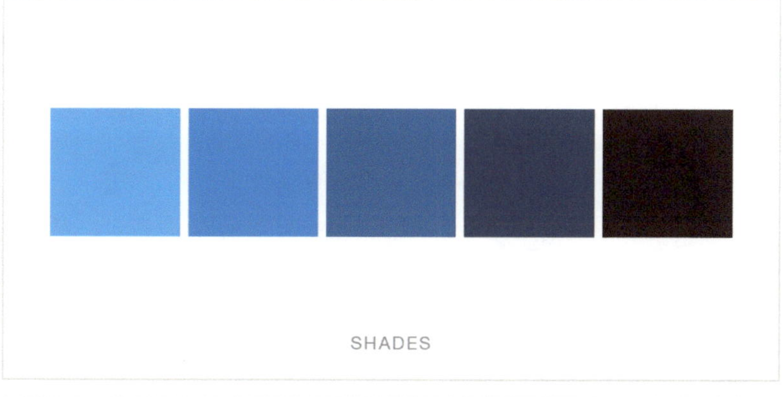

Figure 4-6

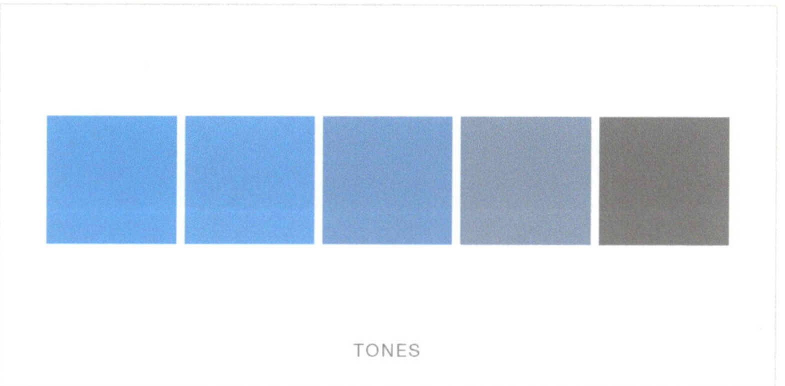

Figure 4-7

the existing hue is diluted, and no additional hues are introduced to the mixture.

Adding white to a hue creates a **tint** of that hue (4-5). Tints are always lighter in value than the original hue. Also known as pastel colors, tints are soft in appearance. Adding black to a hue creates a **shade** of that hue (4-6). Shades are always darker in value than the original hue and possess a deep, rich quality. Adding gray to a hue creates a **tone** of that hue (4-7).

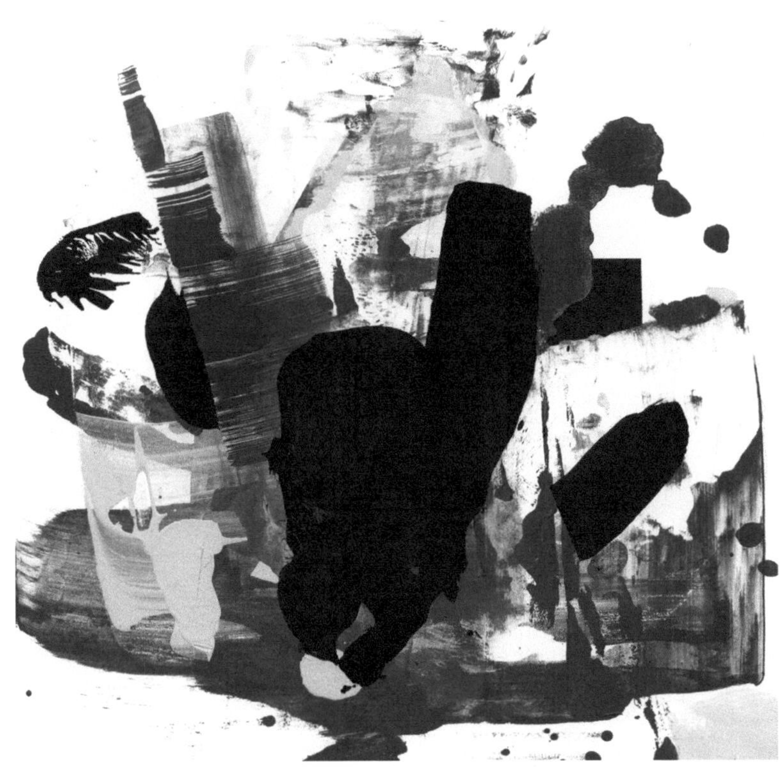

ACHROMATIC COLORS. Vince Contarino, **March / Boris / Riot Sugar**, 2013. Acrylic on paper, 12 x 12 inches. © *Vince Contarino. Courtesy of the artist.*

Depending on the value of the gray being added, tones can be lighter or darker in value than the original hue. Adding gray that is lighter in value than the original hue will create a tone that is lighter in value. Adding gray that is darker in value than the original hue will create a tone that is darker in value. Adding gray that is equal in value to the original hue will create a tone of equal value. While tints, shades, and tones are all specific types of variations that describe changes in value and saturation, the terms are often misused in everyday language to describe slight variations in hue.

5

5 COLOR SYSTEMS

Color is experienced in one of two ways, either directly as projected light or indirectly as reflected light. Color that is experienced directly, as projected light, is classified as **additive** color. Televisions, computer monitors, and theater lighting are all examples of media that utilize additive color mixing. In an additive color system, the absence of color is black with no light being projected. As additive colors are introduced and mixed, the amount of projected light increases, producing colors that are lighter in value. Combining all colors in an additive color system maximizes the amount of projected light and results in white. Color that is experienced indirectly, as reflected light, is classified as **subtractive** color. Paints, inks, and dyes are all examples of media that utilize subtractive color. In a subtractive color system, the absence of color or pigment is white. As subtractive colors are introduced and mixed, the amount of reflected light decreases, producing colors that are darker in value. Combining all colors in a subtractive color system minimizes the amount of reflected light and results in black (5-1).

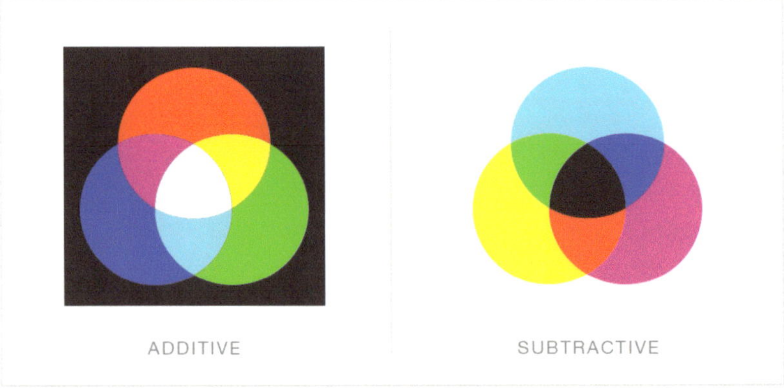

Figure 5-1

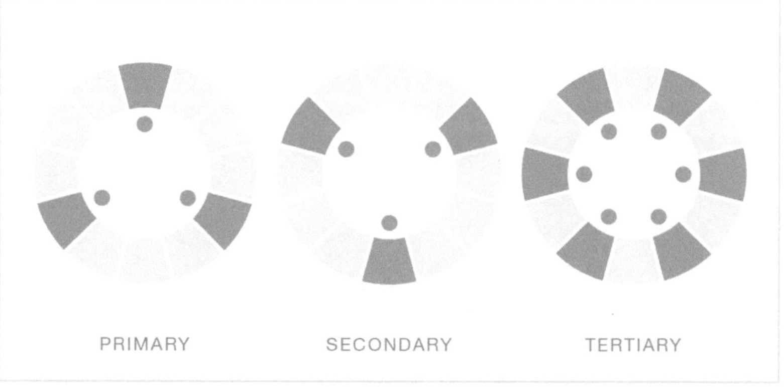

Figure 5-2

In any color system, a hue is considered **primary** if it cannot be obtained through the mixture of other hues. Primary hues are indivisible and cannot be visually separated into other component hues. Every color within a given color system can be derived through a unique combination of its primary hues.

Mixing two primary hues together in equal proportions creates a **secondary** hue. A secondary hue serves as a visual midpoint between two primary hues. Mixing a primary hue with an associated secondary hue creates a **tertiary** hue. A tertiary hue serves as a visual midpoint between a primary and secondary hue.

A **color wheel** is a basic tool that organizes the primary, secondary, and tertiary hues of a color system into a circle. The first step in building a color wheel is to evenly space the primary hues around the perimeter of a circle. Then, the secondary hues are placed on the circle as midpoints between the corresponding primary hues. Finally, the tertiary hues are placed as midpoints between the appropriate primary and secondary hues (5-2). To create a color wheel with more than 12 steps,

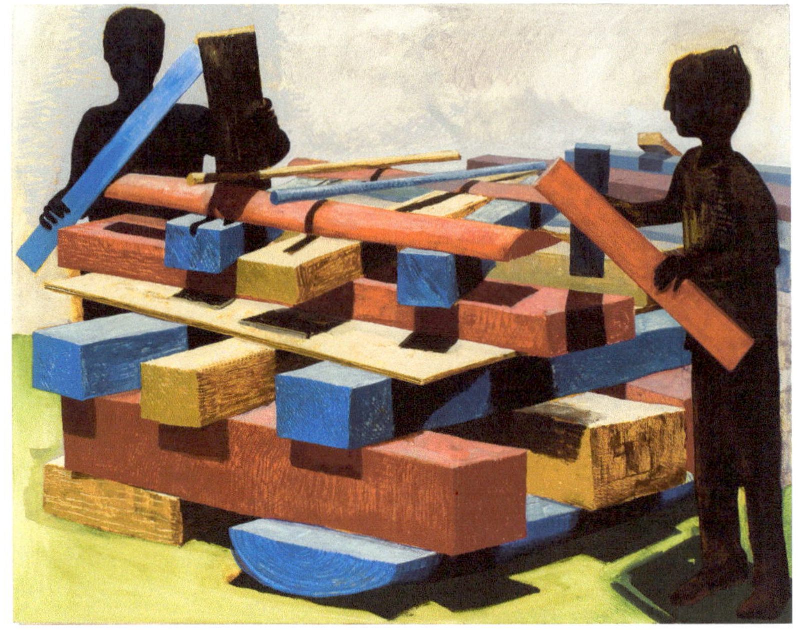

RYB PRIMARIES. Jesse Chapman, **The Collectors**, 2009. Oil on linen, 50 x 62 inches. © *Jesse Chapman. Photography by John Schmid. Courtesy of the artist and Shane Campbell Gallery, Chicago.*

additional intermediate hue mixtures can be placed between each tertiary hue and its neighboring primary or secondary hue. Because there are numerous color systems with differing sets of primary hues, there are also numerous color wheels with differing applications. For the purposes of this text, we will explore three different color systems based on the varying primary hues for paint, light, and color printing.

The primary hues for paint are red, yellow, and blue (5-3). The red, yellow, and blue or **RYB** color system is subtractive and traditionally favored by artists and educators due to the historical importance of paint in art. In theory, mixing all three

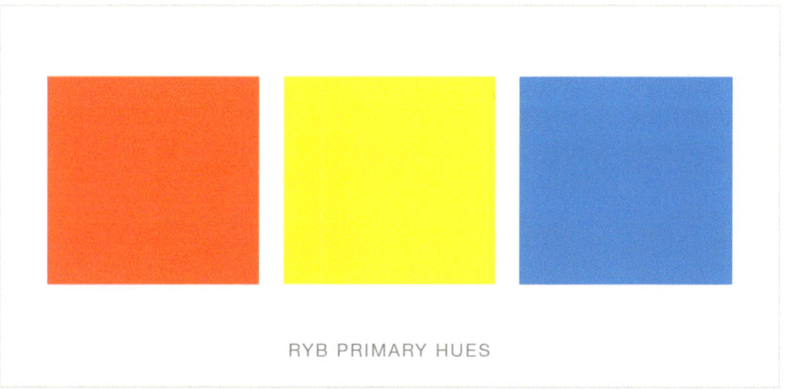

Figure 5-3

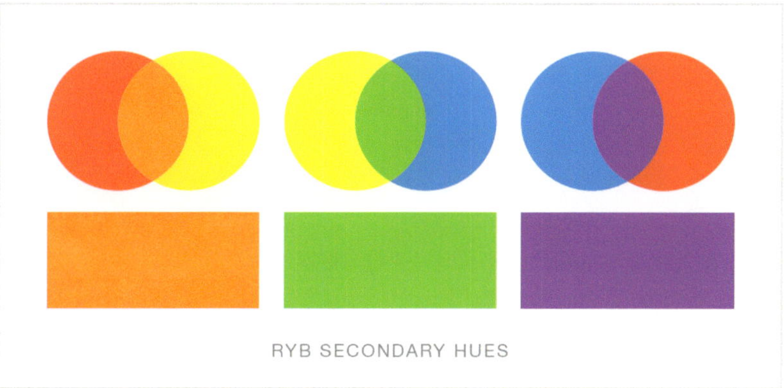

Figure 5-4

paint primaries in equal portions should produce black; however, mixing red, yellow, and blue paints in practice normally produces a dark brown color. In the RYB color system, mixing equal parts of red and yellow produces the secondary hue of orange. Mixing equal parts of yellow and blue produces the secondary hue of green, and mixing equal parts of blue and red produces the secondary hue of violet (5-4). The tertiary hues of the RYB color system are red-orange, yellow-orange,

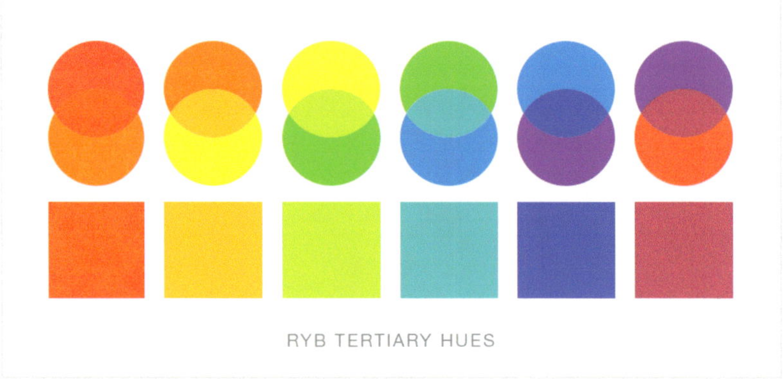

Figure 5-5

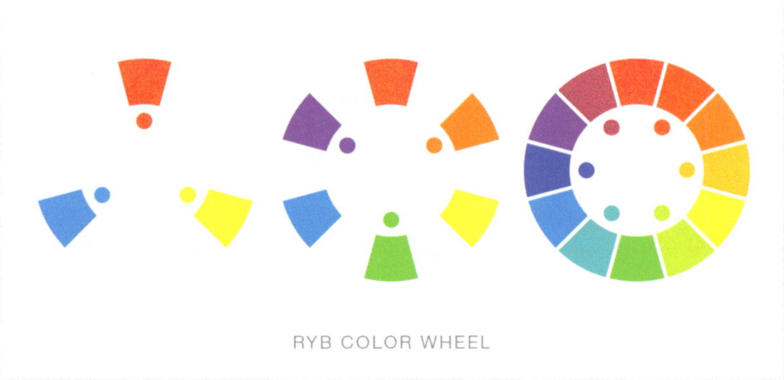

Figure 5-6

yellow-green, blue-green, blue-violet, and red-violet (5-5). The primary, secondary, and tertiary hues for paint can be organized into an RYB color wheel (5-6).

The primary hues of light are red, green, and blue (5-7). The red, green, and blue or **RGB** color system is additive and utilized with digital media such as computer graphics and digital photography. In the RGB color system, combining all three light primaries in equal portions produces white. Mixing equal

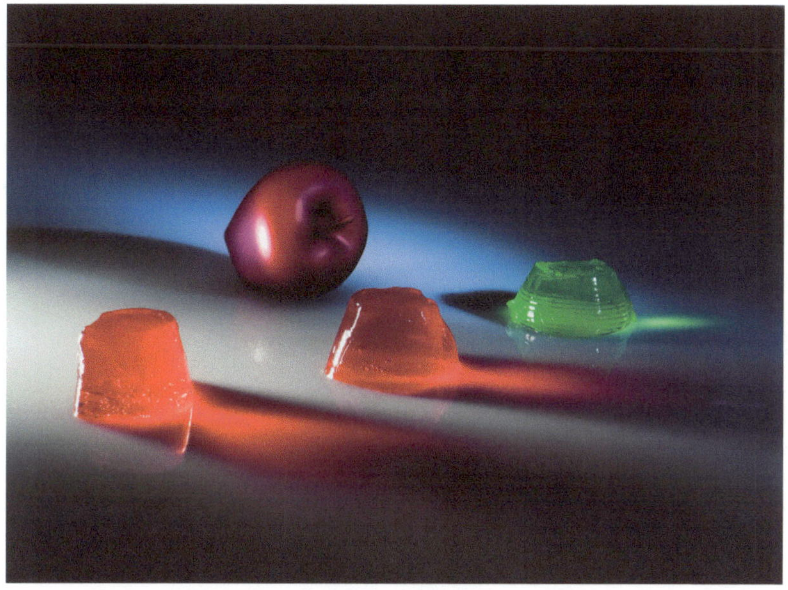

RGB PRIMARIES. Claudia Hart, **RGB**, 2011. Archival inkjet print on photo rag, 36 x 48 inches. © *Claudia Hart. Courtesy of bitforms gallery, New York.*

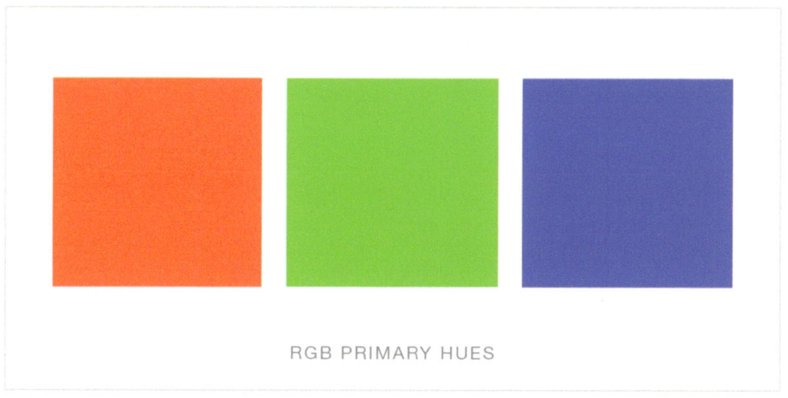

Figure 5-7

parts of red and green produces the secondary hue of yellow, mixing equal parts of green and blue produces the secondary hue of cyan, and mixing equal parts of blue and red produces

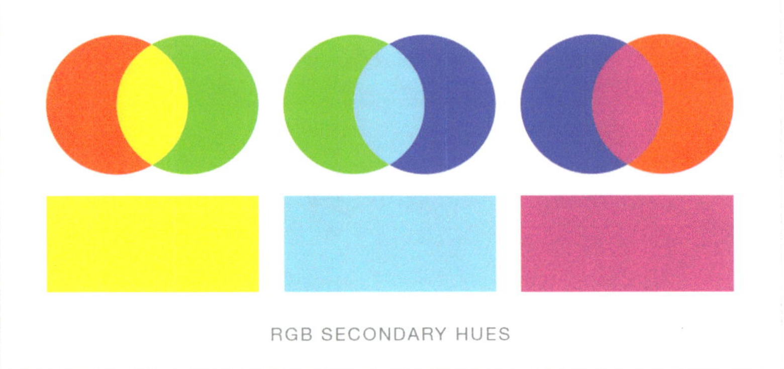

Figure 5-8

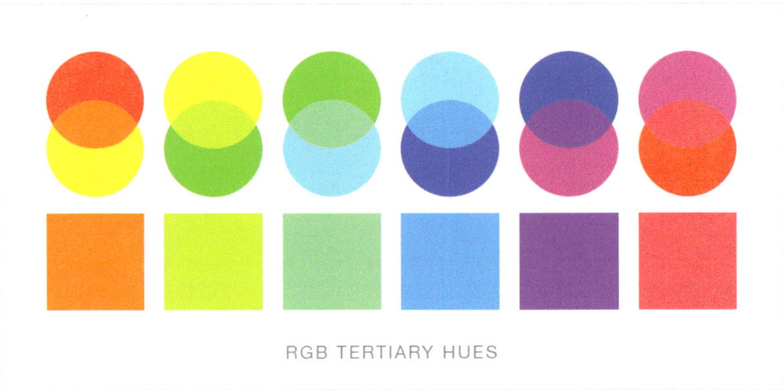

Figure 5-9

the secondary hue of magenta (5-8). The tertiary hues of the RGB color system are orange, yellow-green, cool green, cool blue, violet, and cool red (5-9).

The primary hues for transparent ink are cyan, magenta, and yellow (5-10). Color printing is a subtractive process, so layering all three primary inks in equal portions should produce black. However, layering cyan, magenta, and yellow inks in practice normally produces a dark gray color. Because of this, black ink

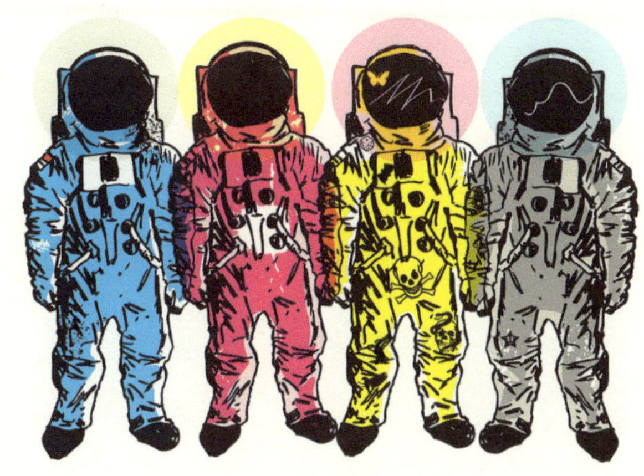

CMYK PRIMARIES. Matt Fontaine, **CMYK Spacemen**, 2012. Vector based design, 11 x 17 inches. © *Matt Fontaine. Courtesy of the artist.*

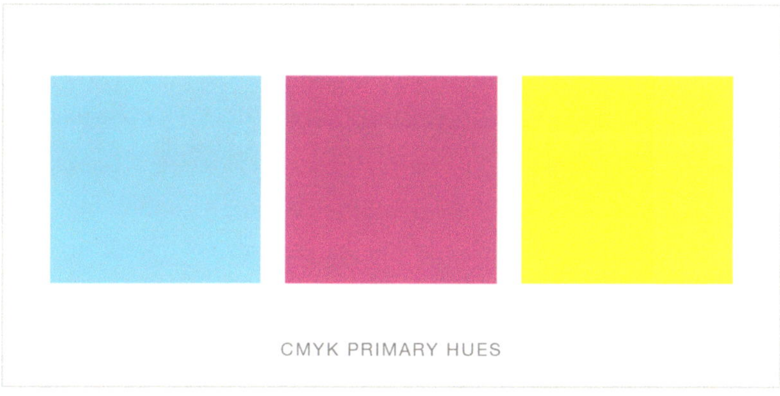

Figure 5-10

is also included in the printing process for achieving true blacks. The color black is abbreviated by the letter K, for key. Key is the term for the final printing pass that provides image detail. In the cyan, magenta, yellow, and black or **CMYK** color system, mixing equal parts of cyan and magenta produces the secondary hue of blue. Mixing equal parts of magenta and yellow produces

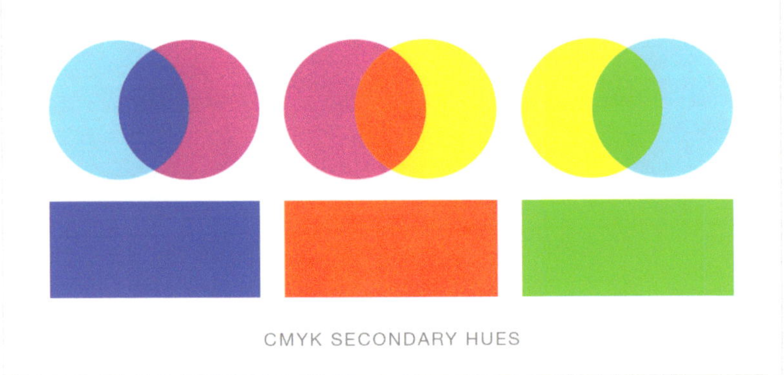

Figure 5-11

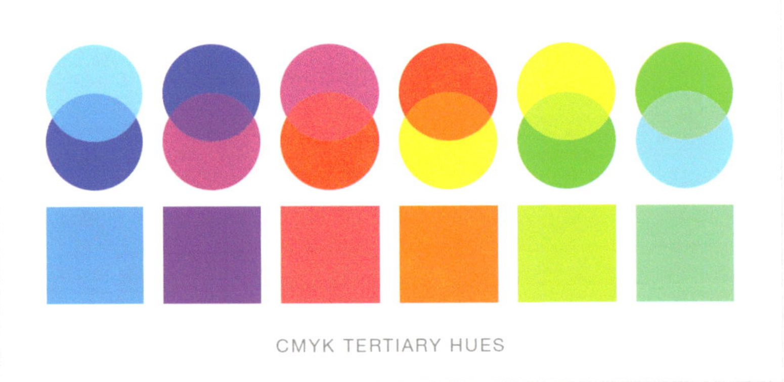

Figure 5-12

the secondary hue of red, and mixing equal parts of yellow and cyan produces the secondary hue of green (5-11). The tertiary hues of the CMYK color system are cool blue, violet, cool red, orange, yellow-green, and cool green (5-12). Colors derived through a combination of cyan, magenta, yellow, and black inks are also known as **process colors**.

It is important to note that the primary hues of the RGB color system are the secondary hues of the CMYK color system,

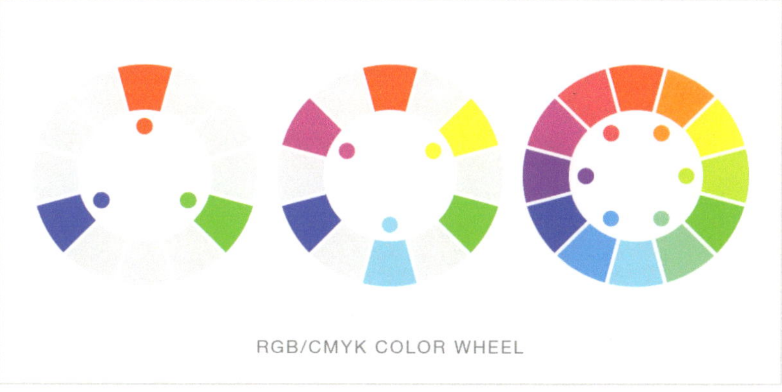

Figure 5-13

and similarly, the primary hues of the CMYK color system are the secondary hues of the RGB color system. Both systems also have the same tertiary hues. Because of this, a single color wheel can be developed for use with both color systems (5-13). The primary and secondary hues are simply reversed depending on the application. The key difference between the RGB and CMYK color systems is the range of colors that can be produced with the primary hues, known as the **gamut** of the color system. The RGB color system has a larger gamut than the CMYK color system, meaning that a wider range of colors with higher saturations can be achieved through RGB mixtures in light than with CMYK mixtures in transparent ink.

COLOR SCHEMES

6

6 COLOR SCHEMES

A selection of colors used for a specific application is known as a **color scheme** or **color palette**. There are endless possibilities, both systematic and intuitive, for developing a color scheme. Logical methods can be established for selecting color combinations, although their success is not automatic and can vary based on individual preferences and cultural influences. On the other hand, artists often work with color intuitively, making spontaneous color choices while they are engaged with the creative process. Regardless of how a color scheme is determined, the primary goal is for the color use to be effective for the given application.

Any combination of colors can have the quality of harmony or dissonance. Color **harmony** suggests a pleasing combination of colors that is ordered and balanced. Color harmony appears purposeful and contributes to the overall unity of a composition. Color **dissonance** suggests a conflicting combination of colors that is unbalanced and chaotic. Depending on the application, color dissonance can be off-putting, or it can be a desired quality that adds energy and excitement (6-1).

Strategies for building color schemes can be developed around any of the defining properties of color. Color schemes based on the property of hue are normally determined by the positions of hues relative to one another on a color wheel. Hues that are near each other on a color wheel are similar in character, while hues that are farther apart have greater contrast. Simple hue relationships tend to be more self-evident, while complex hue relationships are less apparent. In addition to the basic hue relationships outlined in this chapter, more

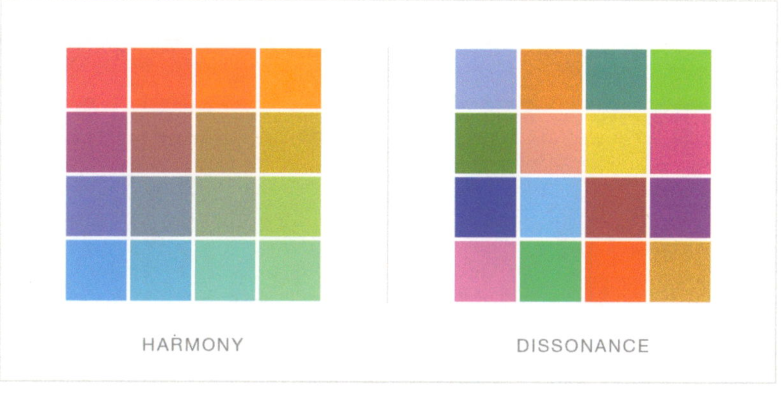

Figure 6-1

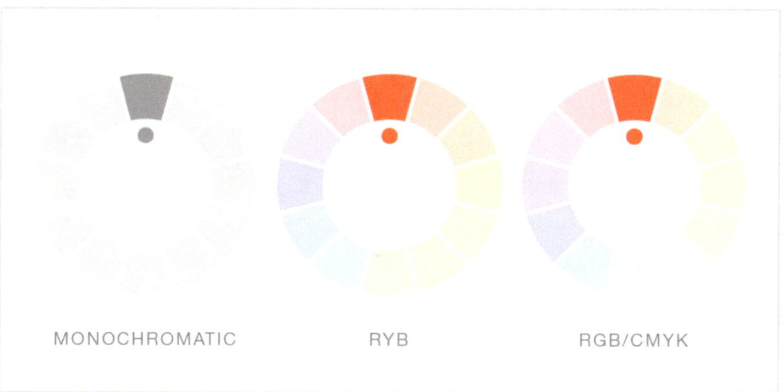

Figure 6-2

intricate or less structured arrangements can be explored for different results. The color wheel being used can also significantly impact how hues are organized and selected for color schemes. This can be seen in the diagram for each hue relationship by comparing its application to both the RYB and RGB/CMYK color wheels.

The simplest use of hue can be found in a **monochromatic** color scheme, which employs a single, fixed hue (6-2).

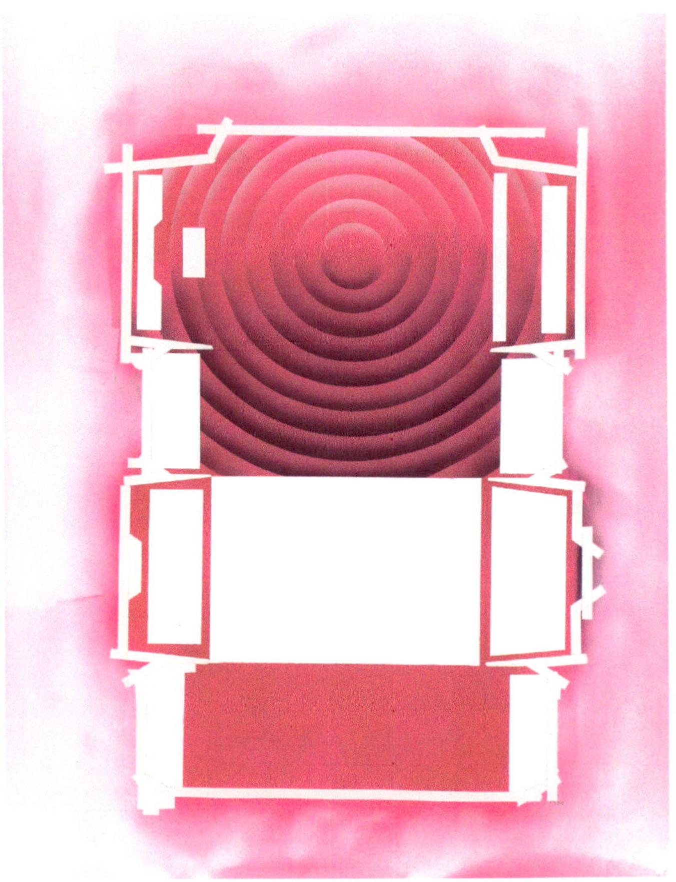

MONOCHROMATIC COLOR. Ester Partegàs, **Studies on Mysticism (Purple Target)**, 2010. Acrylic and graphite on paper, 41 x 31 inches. © Ester Partegàs. Courtesy of Foxy Production, New York.

Monochromatic color schemes have no contrast in hue and variations in value and saturation extend the scheme into additional colors. Through the consistent use of a shared hue, monochromatic color schemes are restrained and balanced.

When multiple hues neighbor each other on a color wheel, they are considered to be **analogous** (6-3). Analogous hues have limited contrast in hue and share a common hue bias.

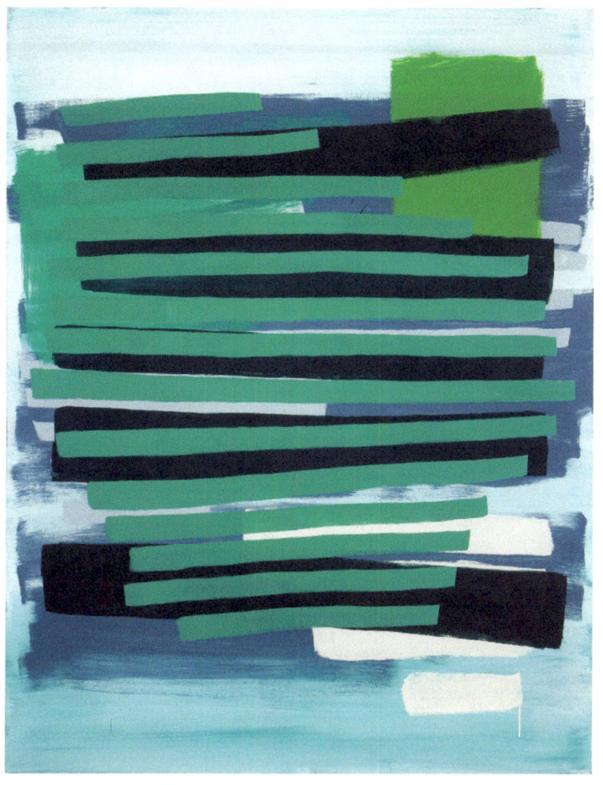

ANALOGOUS HUES. Jon Pestoni, **Green Paragraph**, 2010. Oil on canvas on panel, 64 x 48 inches. © *Jon Pestoni. Courtesy of the artist.*

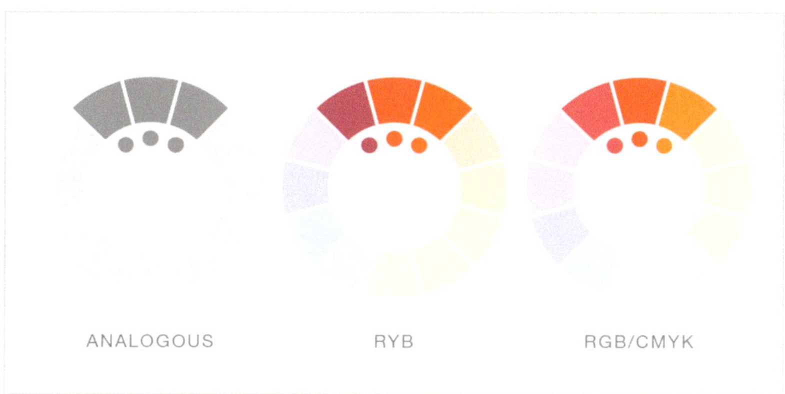

Figure 6-3

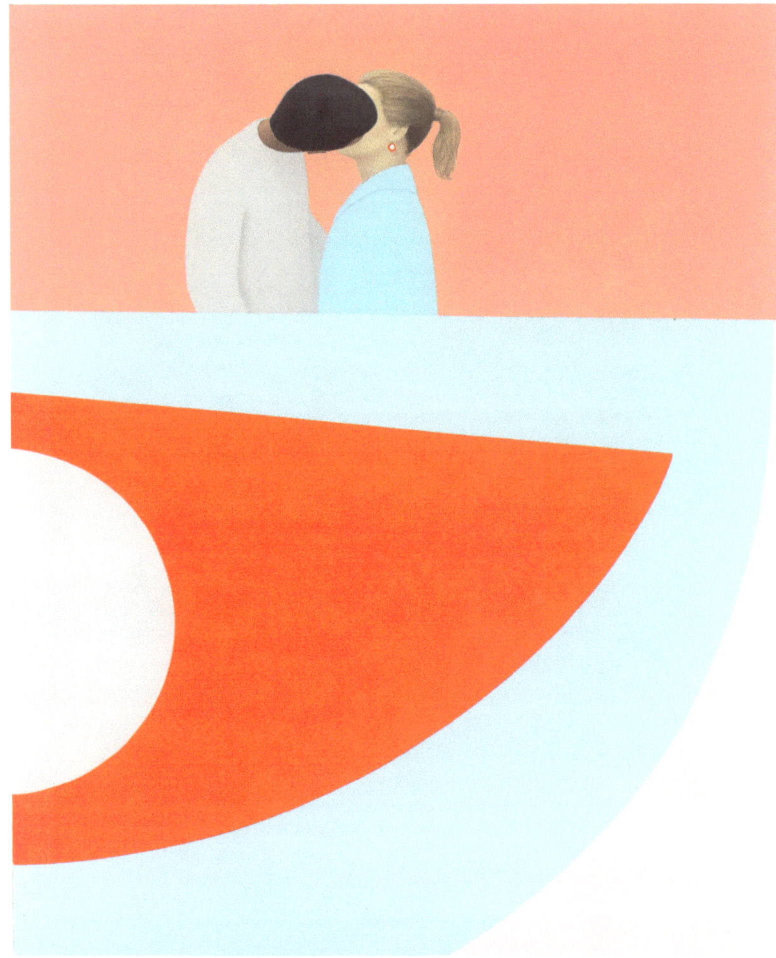

COMPLEMENTARY HUES. Ridley Howard, **Grand Avenue Kiss**, 2014. Oil on linen, 50 x 40 inches. © *Ridley Howard. Photography by Jeffrey Sturges. Courtesy of the artist and Koenig & Clinton, New York.*

Using a controlled section of the color wheel, analogous hue relationships are generally calm and stable.

Two hues that lie directly opposite one another on a color wheel are considered **complementary** (6-4). Complementary hues have maximum contrast in hue and tend to intensify one

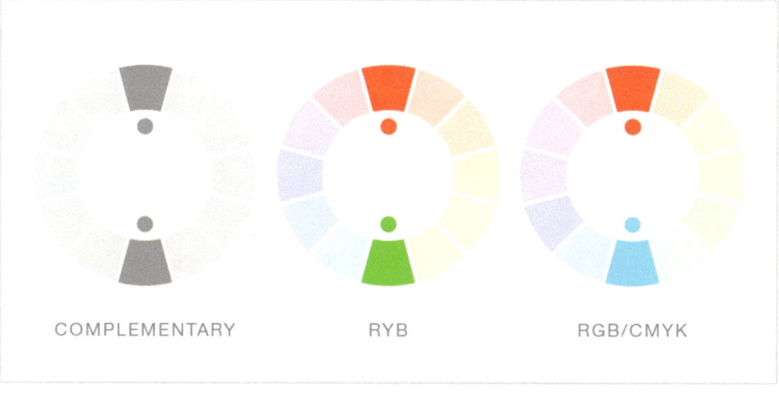

Figure 6-4

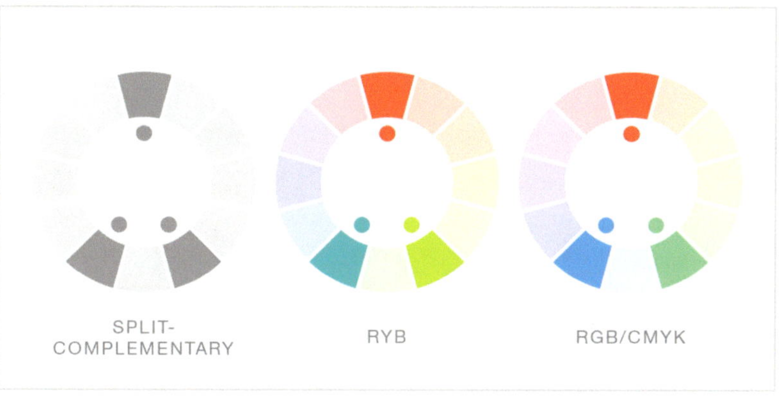

Figure 6-5

another. Because of this, complementary hue relationships are bold and expressive.

A **split-complementary** hue relationship is a variant of a complementary hue relationship. Split-complementary hue relationships replace the hue at one end of a complementary pair with two neighboring hues on the color wheel, one from each side (6-5). Combining properties of both analogous and complementary hue relationships, split-complementary hue

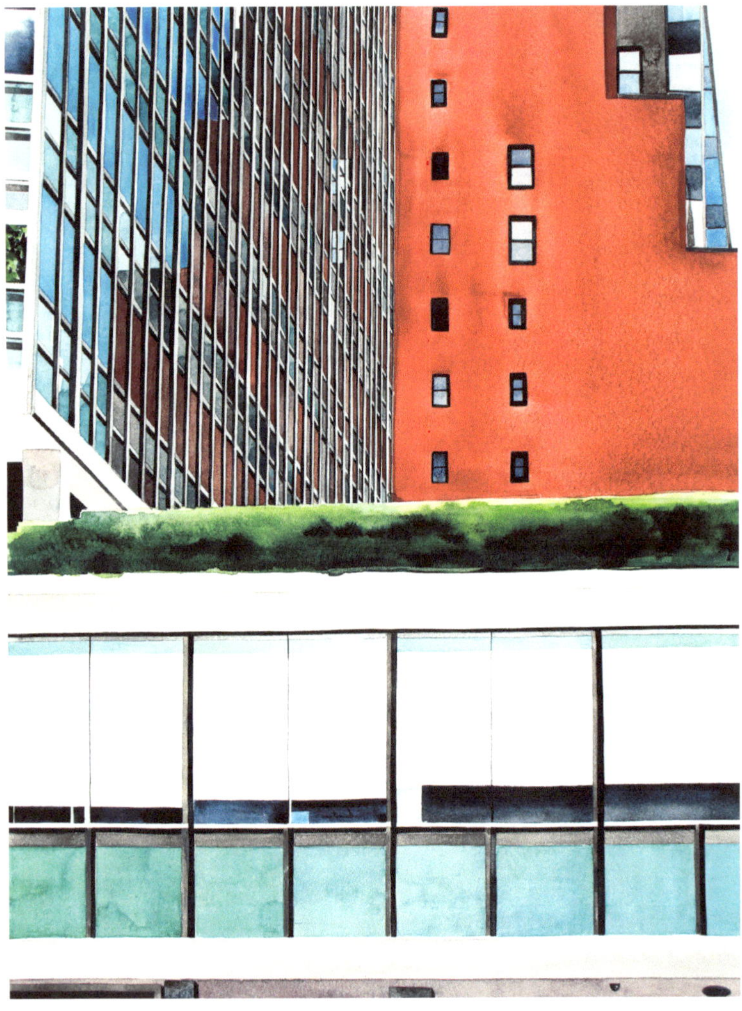

SPLIT-COMPLEMENTARY HUES. Amy Park, **Lever House, NYC**, 2013. Watercolor on paper, 30 x 22 inches. © *Amy Park. Photography by James Pakola. Courtesy of Morgan Lehman Gallery.*

relationships are more diverse and less extreme than using true complements.

A **double-complementary** hue relationship utilizes two sets of complementary hues. Double-complementary hue relationships

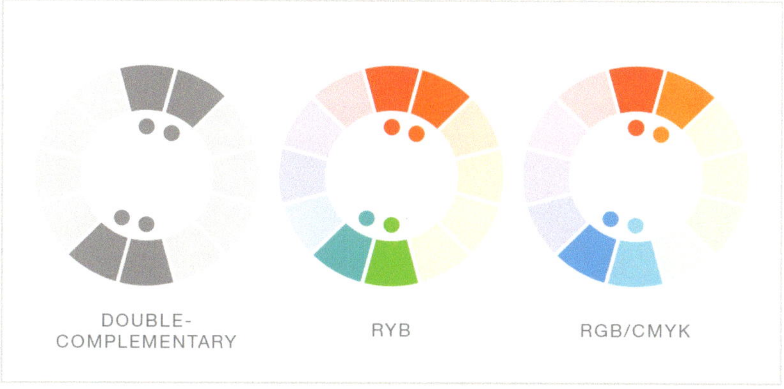

Figure 6-6

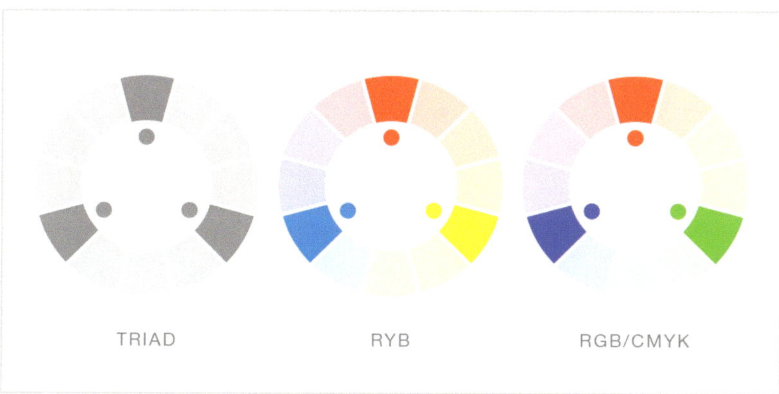

Figure 6-7

are usually constructed from two adjacent hues on the color wheel combined with their corresponding complementary hues (6-6). Double-complementary hue relationships share the same expressive qualities as complementary hues, but allow the use of more than two hues.

Three hues that are equidistant from one another on the color wheel have a **triad** relationship (6-7). Triad hue relationships exhibit the maximum contrast between three different hues.

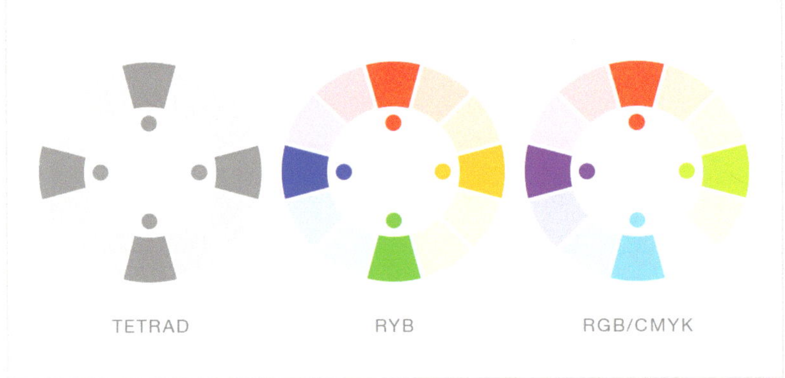

Figure 6-8

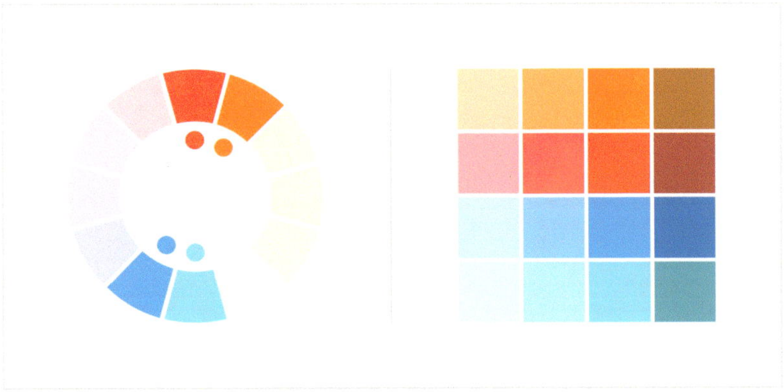

Figure 6-9

Triad hue relationships provide equilibrium and balance with moderate contrast.

Four hues that are equidistant from one another on the color wheel have a **tetrad** relationship (6-8). Tetrad hue relationships exhibit the maximum contrast between four different hues. A tetrad hue relationship can also be viewed as a specialized double-complementary relationship, utilizing two opposing pairs of complementary hues. Like triad relationships, tetrad

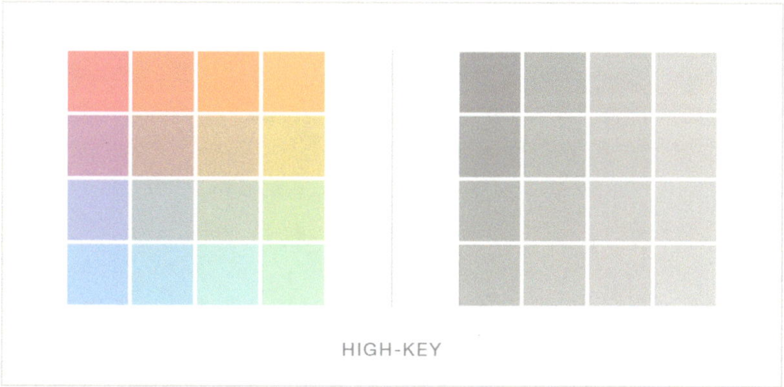

Figure 6-10

hue relationships provide equilibrium and balance but with slightly less overall contrast.

Any hue relationship can be developed into a full color scheme by including tints, tones, and shades of the selected hues (6-9). This provides variation in value and saturation and expands the color scheme beyond the use of fully saturated hues. White, black, and achromatic grays can be added to any color scheme without affecting the hue relationship.

In addition to hue, color schemes can also be developed around the property of value. Color schemes can be organized by a tendency towards light, medium, or dark values or by controlling the overall range in value.

A high-key color scheme emphasizes light values. **High-key** values range from white to light gray on the value scale (6-10). Color schemes using high-key values are soft and delicate.

An intermediate-key color scheme emphasizes medium values. **Intermediate-key** values sit between light gray and dark gray

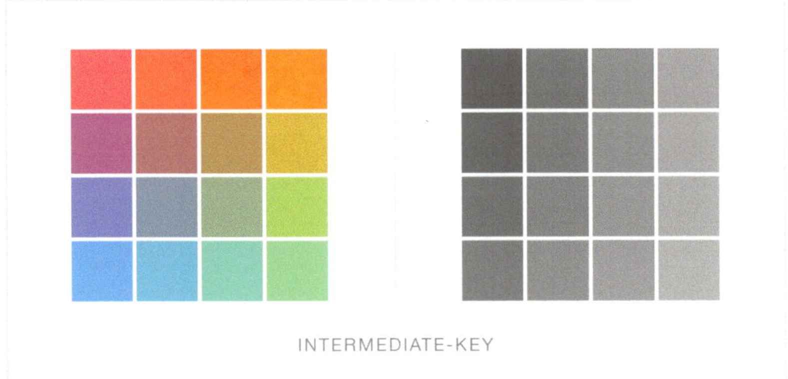

INTERMEDIATE-KEY

Figure 6-11

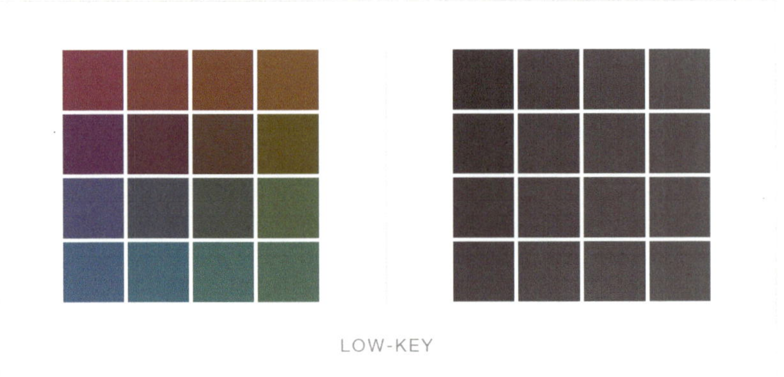

LOW-KEY

Figure 6-12

on the value scale (6-11). Color schemes using intermediate-key values are generally stable and allow the use of fully saturated hues.

A low-key color scheme emphasizes dark values. **Low-key** values range from dark gray to black on the value scale (6-12). Color schemes using low-key values tend to be heavy and ominous.

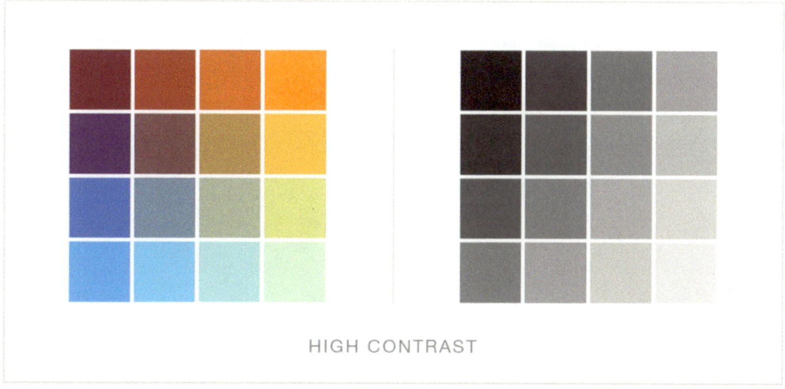

Figure 6-13

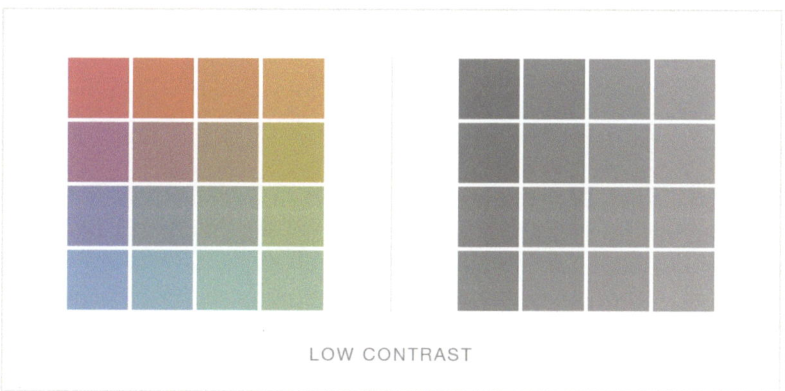

Figure 6-14

A color scheme that utilizes a wide range of dissimilar values is considered high contrast. Values with high contrast are far apart from one another on the value scale (6-13). High contrast color schemes provide impact and clarity.

A color scheme that utilizes a narrow range of similar values is considered low contrast. Values with low contrast are near one another on the value scale (6-14). Low contrast color schemes are usually quiet and introspective.

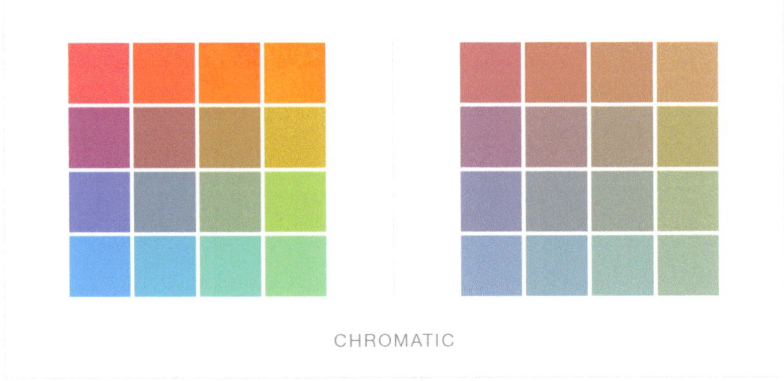

Figure 6-15

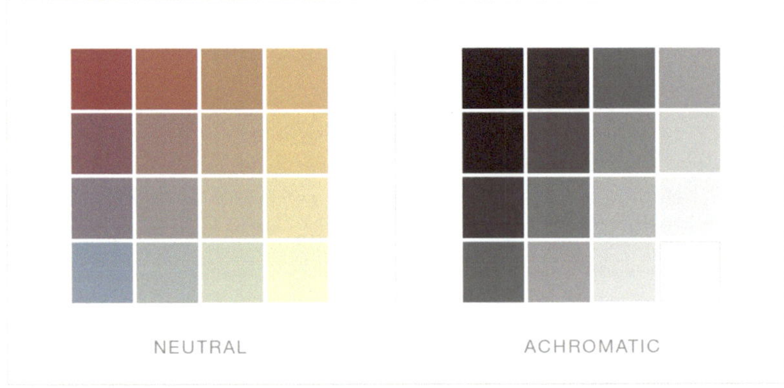

Figure 6-16

Furthermore, color schemes can also be developed around the property of saturation. Color schemes can be constructed with a tendency towards strong, moderate, or weak saturation levels or limited to only achromatic colors. Chromatic color schemes emphasize either strong or moderate saturation levels. Chromatic color schemes with strong saturation levels are bright and active, while chromatic color schemes with

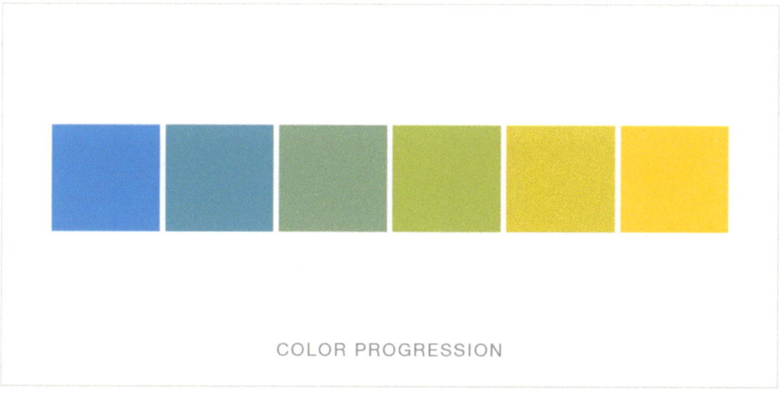

Figure 6-17

moderate saturation levels are less aggressive overall (6-15). Neutral color schemes emphasize low saturation levels and are generally more subdued. Finally, achromatic color schemes have no saturation whatsoever and consist only of white, black, and achromatic grays. Achromatic color schemes have no indication of hue and vary only in value (6-16).

While color schemes are usually organized around the defining properties of hue, value and saturation, another way of relating colors is through the use of a color progression. A **color progression** is a series of even visual steps between any two colors. A color progression serves as a bridge between two parent colors and provides an orderly way of linking those colors together into a color scheme (6-17). Color progressions can step through changes in hue, value, or saturation, or any combination of those properties. The number of intermediate steps between parent colors is also variable. A **gradient** is a special type of color progression where the transition in color is continuous, eliminating any discrete steps between the

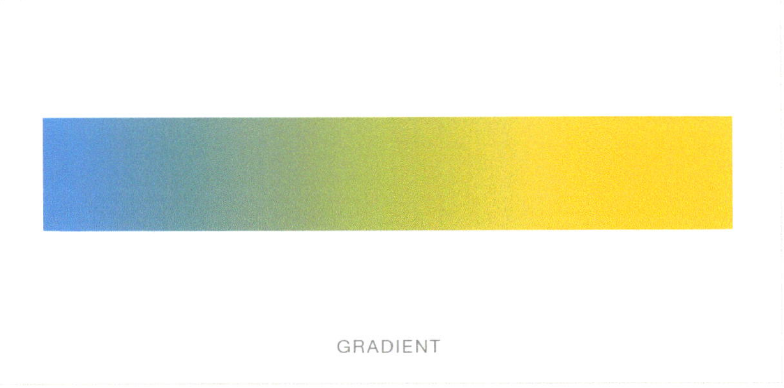

Figure 6-18

parent colors. A gradient provides a smooth blend between two colors and is often used to suggest shading or three-dimensional volume (6-18).

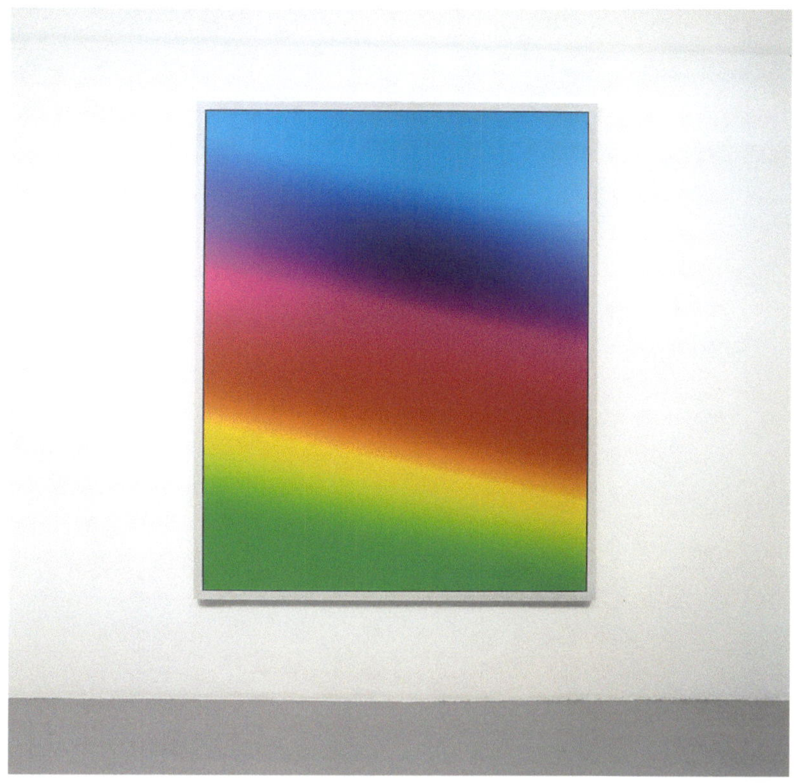

GRADIENT. Cory Arcangel. **Photoshop CS: 84 by 66 inches, 300 DPI, RGB, square pixels, default gradient "Spectrum", mousedown y=3200 x=10200, mouseup y=22600 x=6200**. 2009. Chromogenic print. 84 x 66 in. © *Cory Arcangel. Image courtesy of Cory Arcangel and Lisson Gallery.*

COLOR INTERACTION

7

7   COLOR INTERACTION

In the visible world, a color is never experienced in isolation. Colors are always seen in relation to one another and to their surroundings. Our perception of a single color is strongly influenced by its context and its interaction with other colors, making color a relative and mutable visual quality. To make effective decisions concerning the application of color, one must learn how to predict and control the visual effects caused through the interaction of color.

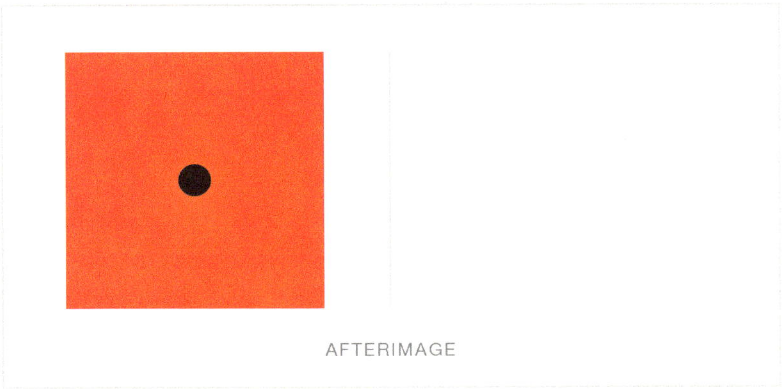

Figure 7-1

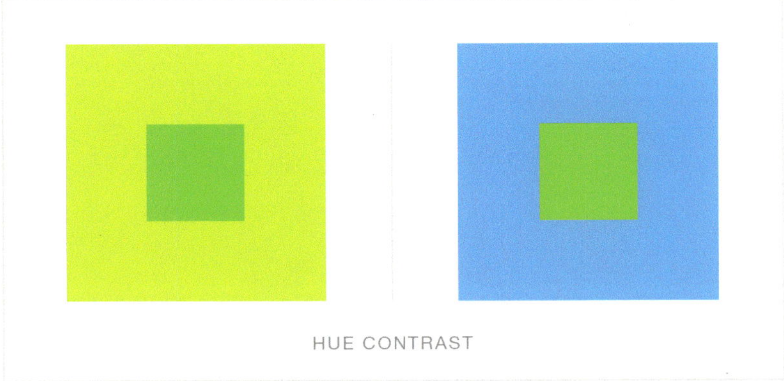

Figure 7-2

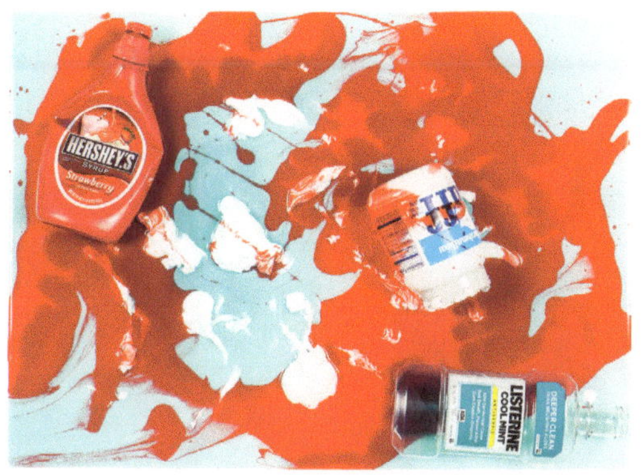

SIMULTANEOUS CONTRAST. Tony Tasset, **Artificial Kills**, 2014. Resin and mixed media on panel, 18 x 24 x 5 inches. © *Tony Tasset. Photography by Joseph Rynkiewicz. Courtesy of Kavi Gupta Gallery.*

An important concept in understanding color relativity is after-image. As the term suggests, an **afterimage** is an image that is perceived after a visual stimulus is removed from our field of vision. Afterimages appear in complementary hues, opposing values, and similar saturations when compared to the original stimulus, much like photographic negatives (7-1). Afterimages occur due to eye fatigue from prolonged visual stimulation: the greater the fatigue, the stronger the afterimage. Afterimages cause us to perceive colors that are not physically present, leading to changes in our color perception.

How a color is perceived is also greatly influenced by its context. When one color is placed on top of another color, the contrast between the two colors decreases their similarities and increases their differences. This apparent shift in color is known as **simultaneous contrast**. Simultaneous contrast can affect any of the defining properties of color. In terms of hue, a background color will both subtract its own hue and add its complementary hue to a surrounded color (7-2). Similarly, a warm background makes a surrounded color appear cooler,

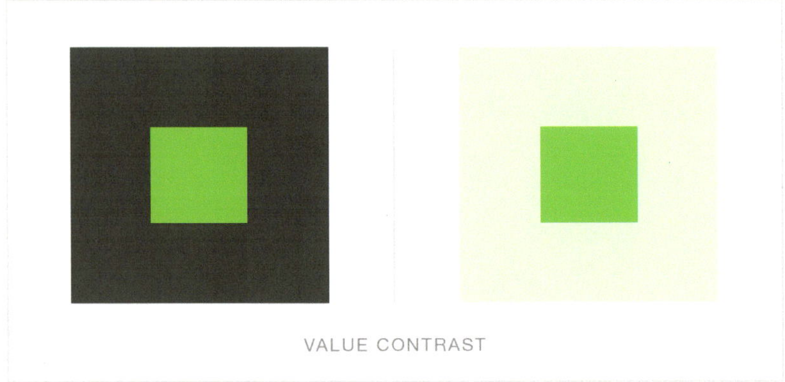

VALUE CONTRAST

Figure 7-3

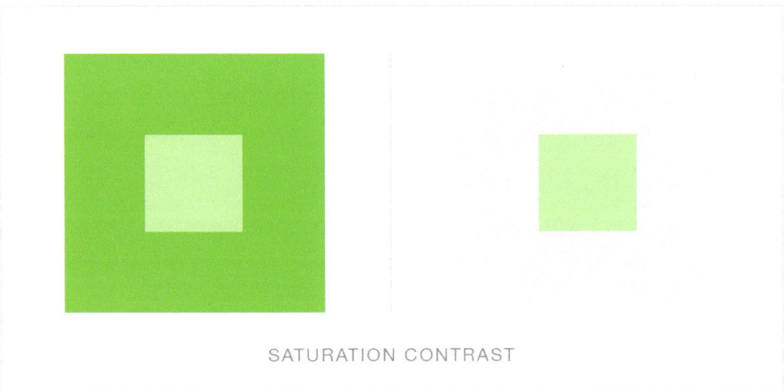

SATURATION CONTRAST

Figure 7-4

while a cool background makes a surrounded color appear warmer. In terms of value, a dark background makes a surrounded color appear lighter while a light background makes a surrounded color appear darker (7-3). In terms of saturation, a bright background makes a surrounded color appear duller while a dull background makes a surrounded color appear brighter (7-4). Furthermore, colors with complementary hues make one another appear brighter and more intense (7-5).

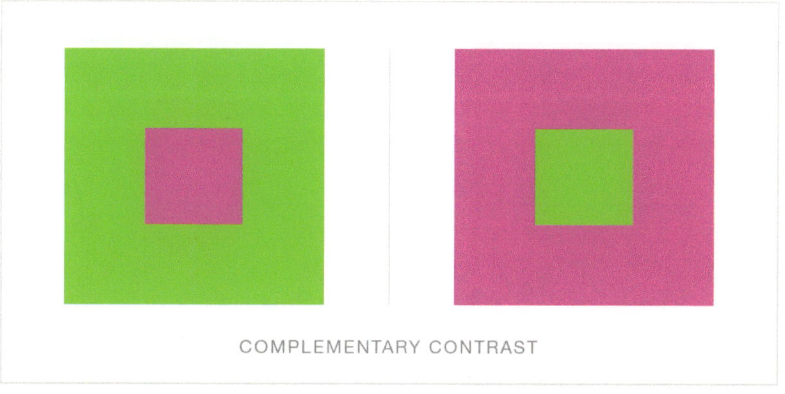

COMPLEMENTARY CONTRAST

Figure 7-5

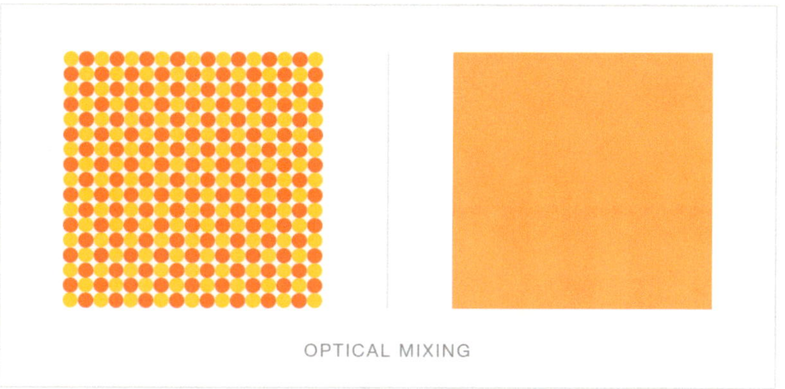

OPTICAL MIXING

Figure 7-6

Another effect that arises through color interaction is optical mixing. In **optical mixing**, small areas of color appear to blend visually to form a new color (7-6). This effect is opposite to simultaneous contrast. Instead of emphasizing the differences between neighboring colors, optical mixing averages their similarities. For optical mixing to occur, the colored areas must be sufficiently small in size, and must be seen from an appropriate distance.

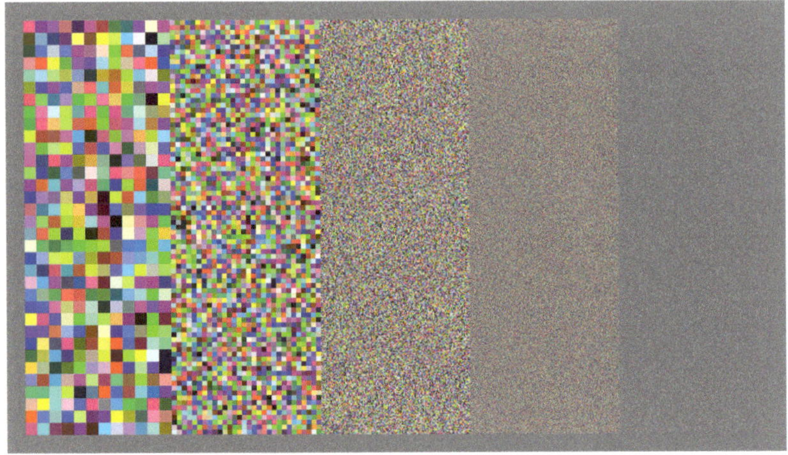

OPTICAL MIXING. Rafael Lozano-Hemmer, **Method Random 1**, 2014.
Chromogenic prints on Kodak Endura paper, 32.2 x 55.22 inches.
© *Rafael Lozano-Hemmer. Courtesy of bitforms gallery, New York.*

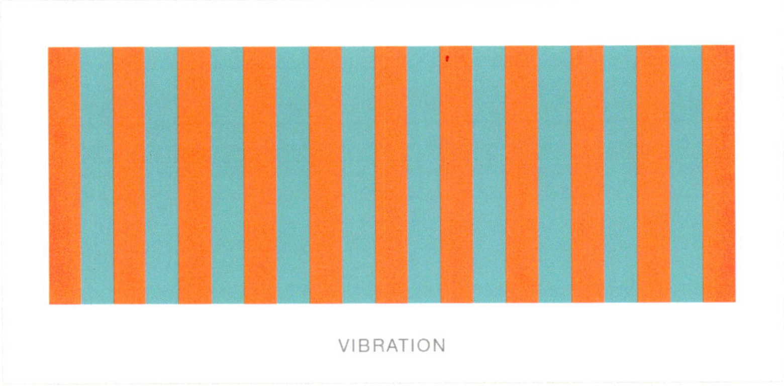

Figure 7-7

Other optical effects can occur along the boundaries where colors meet. **Color vibration** describes a visual experience where the edges between colors appear to shimmer and vibrate. Color vibration occurs when neighboring colors have contrasting hues, similar values, and high saturations (7-7). While color vibration is energetic and exciting, it is also

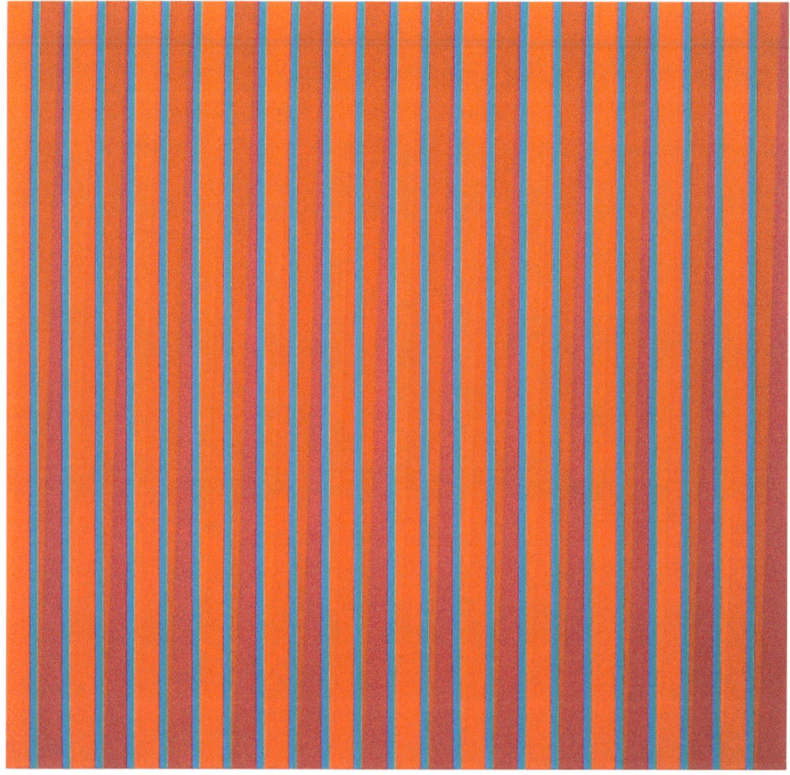

COLOR VIBRATION. Gabriele Evertz, **Four Red bg**, 2002. Acrylic on canvas, 48 x 48 inches. © *Gabriele Evertz. Courtesy of the artist and David Richard Gallery.*

uncomfortable to view for extended periods of time. For this reason, color vibration is often used sparingly or avoided altogether. Color vibration can be diminished in neighboring colors by decreasing their hue contrast, increasing their value contrast, reducing their saturation levels, or by separating the colors to eliminate direct interaction.

A somewhat opposite effect to color vibration is vanishing boundaries. **Vanishing boundaries** is a visual experience where the edges between colors become indistinct and

VANISHING BOUNDARIES. Zak Prekop, **Untitled Transparency with Colors**, 2012. Oil and paper on canvas, 84 x 57 inches. © *Zak Prekop. Courtesy of the artist and Thomas Duncan Gallery, Los Angeles.*

difficult to discern. Vanishing boundaries occur when adjacent colors are both similar in hue and value (7-8).

In addition to color vibration and vanishing boundaries, fluting is another optical effect that occurs along the edges of

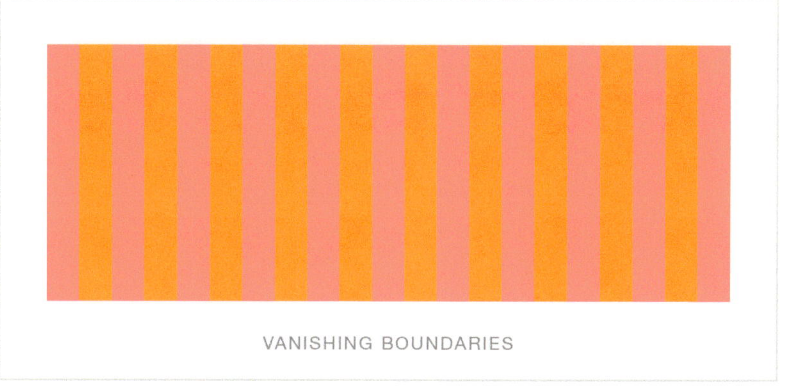

Figure 7-8

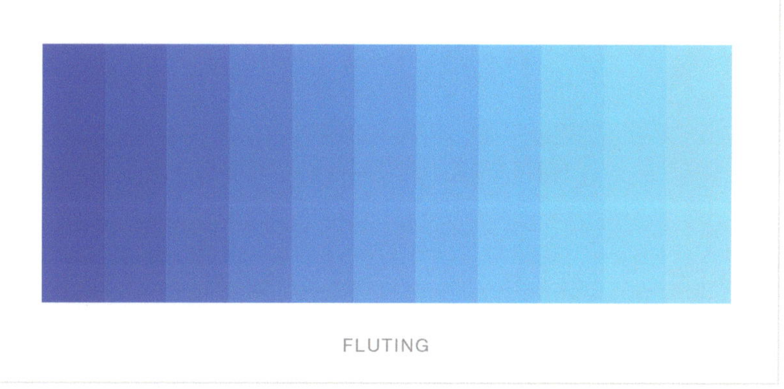

Figure 7-9

colors. **Fluting** usually arises in a sequence of successive color steps, such as a color progression. At the immediate edge between two colors, the effect of simultaneous contrast is strongest. Moving away from the edge, the effect of simultaneous contrast fades. This creates the illusion of a gradient across the surface of the color and suggests a sense of roundness. Repeating this effect over multiple steps creates the appearance of fluting similar to grooves in an architectural column (7-9).

COLOR COMPOSITION

8

8   COLOR COMPOSITION

Color plays a vital role in organizing a composition. As a visual quality, it strongly influences all principles of design. Color can establish contrast and provide emphasis, or it can be used to create balance. Color also helps define space and suggest movement, and it impacts the sense of unity in a composition.

The amount of contrast between two colors is measured by the differences between their defining properties. Contrast can exist in any combination of hue, value, or saturation: the greater the overall difference, the stronger the contrast (8-1). Contrast in color, especially contrast in value, helps define edges and distinguish shapes in a composition.

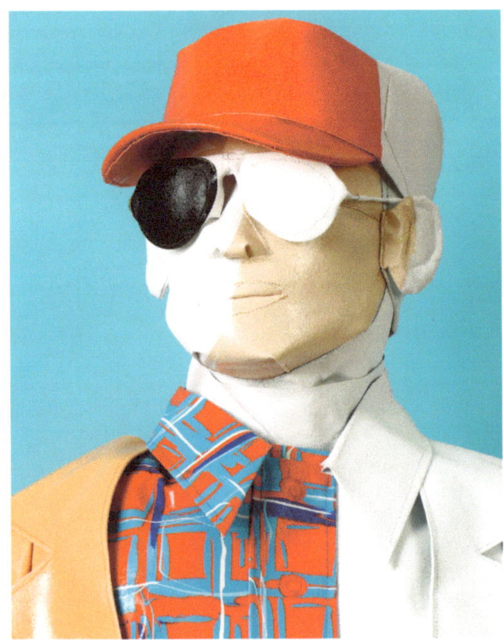

CONTRAST. Boo Ritson, **Scott**, 2010. Archival digital print 1/1, 39 x 30 inches. © Boo Ritson. Courtesy of BravinLee Programs, NY.

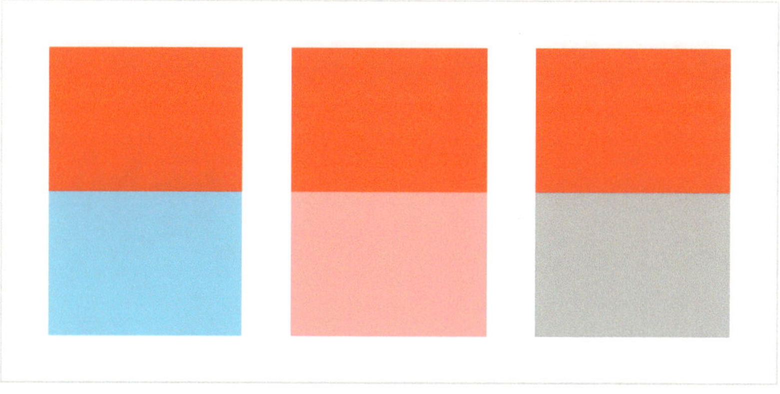

Figure 8-1

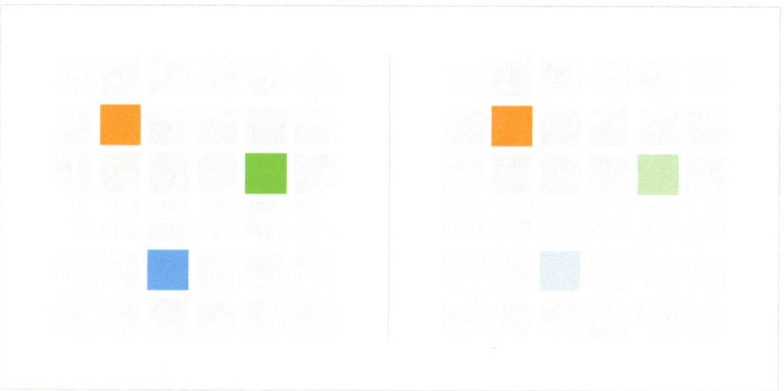

Figure 8-2

Because color immediately attracts our attention, it has a major role in establishing emphasis in a composition. Color can highlight important elements and create focal points in a design. Areas of high color contrast or strong saturation command our attention and are emphasized in a composition, while areas of low color contrast or reduced saturation are less prominent and provide visual rest. Variations in emphasis, from strong to weak, create a hierarchy that guides a viewer's exploration of a composition (8-2).

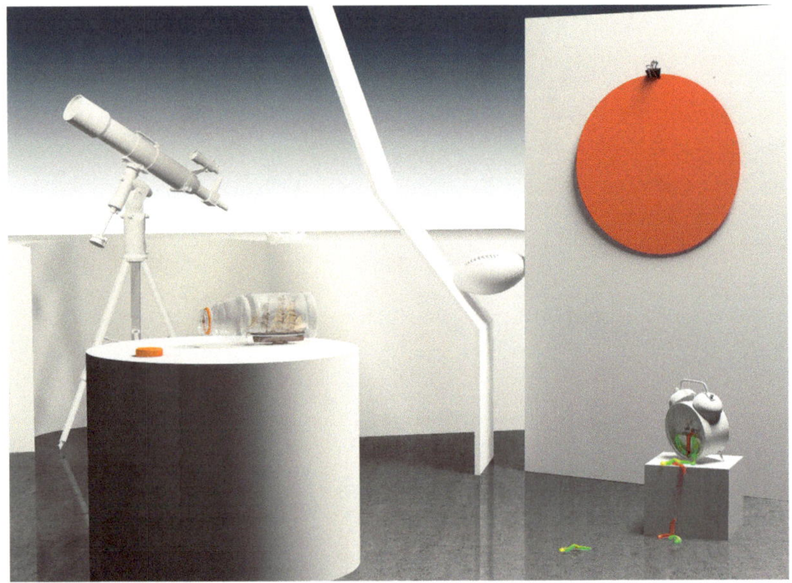

EMPHASIS. Takeshi Murata, **Electrolyte**, 2012. Pigment print, 63.5 x 85 inches. © *Takeshi Murata. Courtesy of the artist; Ratio 3, San Francisco; and Salon 94, New York.*

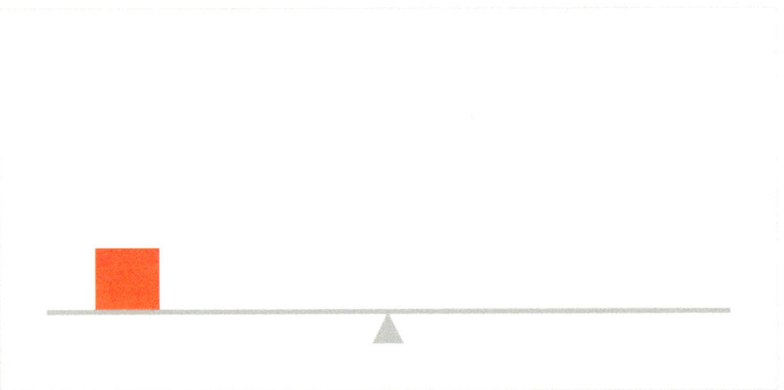

Figure 8-3

Color also significantly impacts the overall balance of a composition. Because areas of high color contrast or strong saturation are more pronounced in a composition, they assume greater

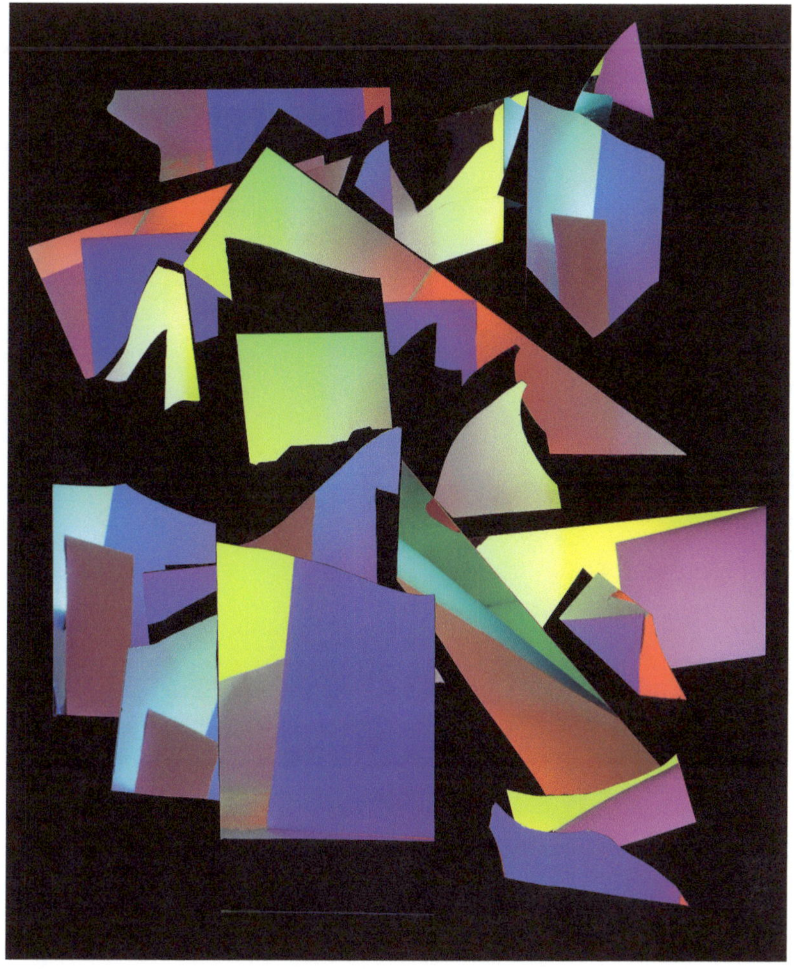

BALANCE. Jessica Labatte, **Untitled_1**, 2012. archival inkjet print, 71.5 x 56.75 inches. © *Jessica Labatt. Courtesy of the artist.*

visual weight than areas of low color contrast or weak saturation. Large areas of low contrast or saturation can then provide balance to small areas of high contrast or saturation (8-3). The distribution of color within a composition also affects balance independently from other design properties. A symmetrical application of color can help balance an asymmetrical

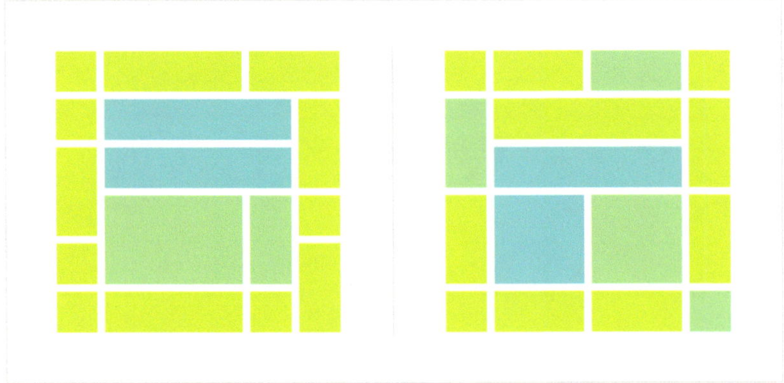

Figure 8-4

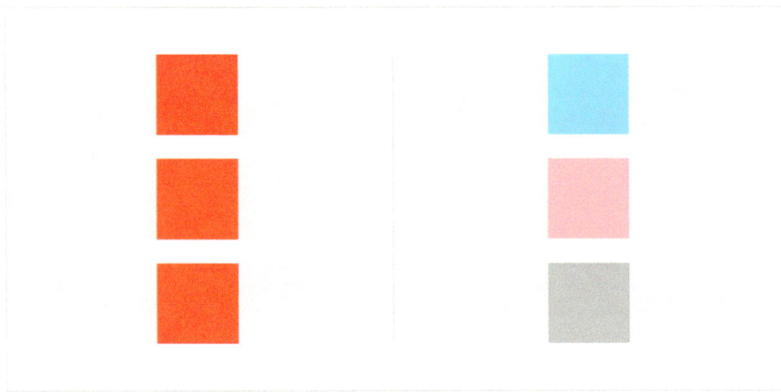

Figure 8-5

arrangement of forms, while an asymmetrical use of color can add visual interest to a symmetrical arrangement of forms (8-4).

The use of color in a composition influences our perception of space as well. Each defining property of color has a different impact on the illusion of depth. In terms of hue, warm hues appear to advance, while cool hues appear to recede. In terms of value, areas of high contrast appear to advance, while

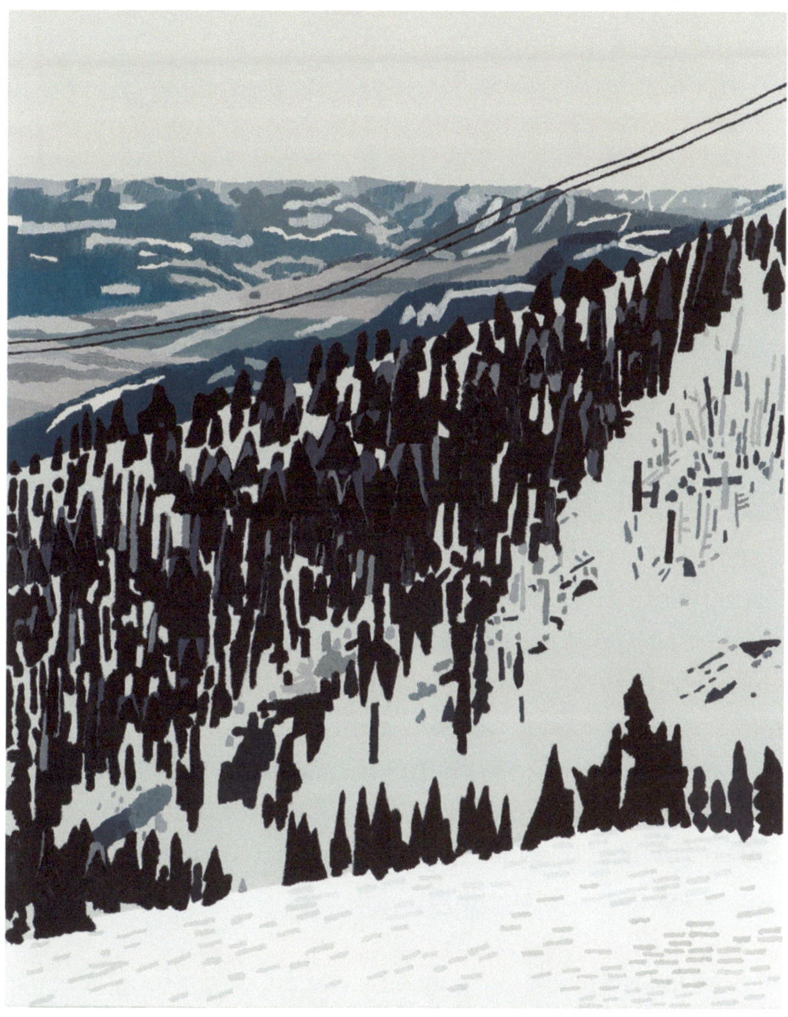

DEPTH. Jonas Wood, **Jackson Hole Wyoming**, 2013. Oil and acrylic on linen, 35 x 27 inches. © Jonas Wood. Photography by Robert Chase Heishman. Courtesy of the artist; Shane Campbell Gallery, Chicago; Anton Kern Gallery, New York; David Kordansky Gallery, Los Angeles.

areas of low contrast appear to recede. In terms of saturation, bright colors appear to advance while muted colors appear to recede (8-5).

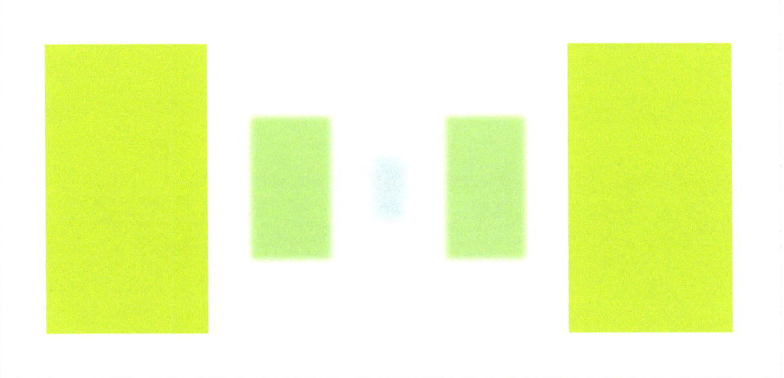

Figure 8-6

Aerial or atmospheric perspective combines the spatial tendencies of hue, value, and saturation to emphasize the sense of depth in a composition. This technique is based on changes in color and contrast that occur when viewing distant objects through a layer of atmosphere and is commonly seen in landscape images. In **aerial** or **atmospheric perspective**, foreground elements are in sharp focus and appear warm in hue, distinct in value, and strong in saturation. Conversely, background elements appear blurry, cool in hue, uniform in value, and weak in saturation (8-6).

A more limited illusion of space can be created through the use of transparency. An illusion of transparency is created when the visual mixture of two or more overlapping colors is placed in the shared region between those colors. Placing an equal visual mixture of the parent colors in the overlapping region will create an ambiguous spatial situation, with no parent color appearing to come forward. But if the overlapping mixture is biased towards one of the parent colors, that color will advance and appear to sit on top of the other colors (8-7).

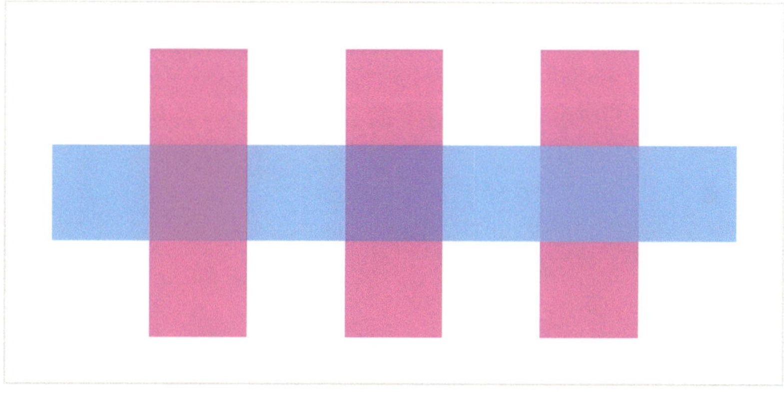

Figure 8-7

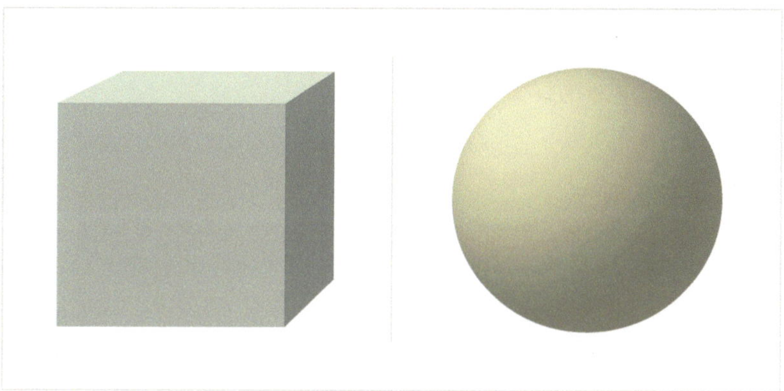

Figure 8-8

Color also significantly contributes to the illusion of volume in a composition. Using variations in value while maintaining a consistent hue simulates the way light falls on three-dimensional objects. Light values suggest highlights, while dark values suggest shadows. Intermediate values suggest mid-tones, which connect areas of highlight and shadow to complete the shading effect. Distinct regions of value suggest flat surfaces, while gradients in value suggest curved surfaces (8-8).

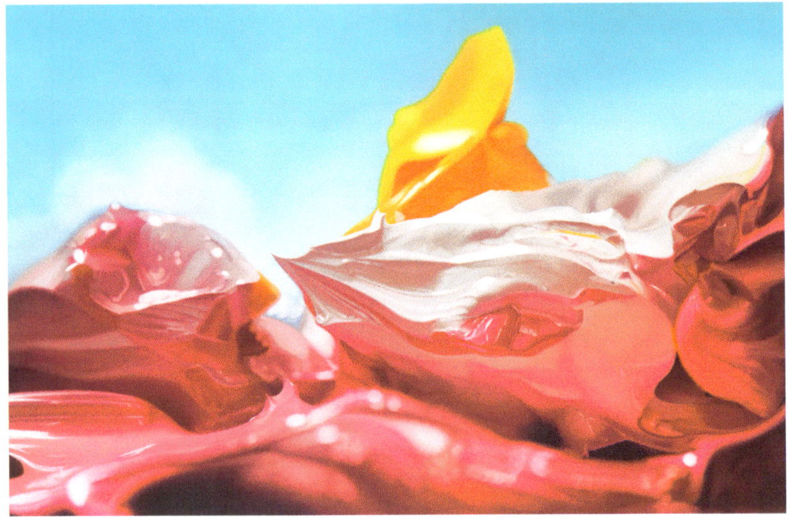

VOLUME. Ben Weiner, **Shrine**, 2012. Oil on canvas, 52 x 78 inches.
© *Ben Weiner and Mark Moore Gallery. Courtesy of the artist and*
Mark Moore Gallery.

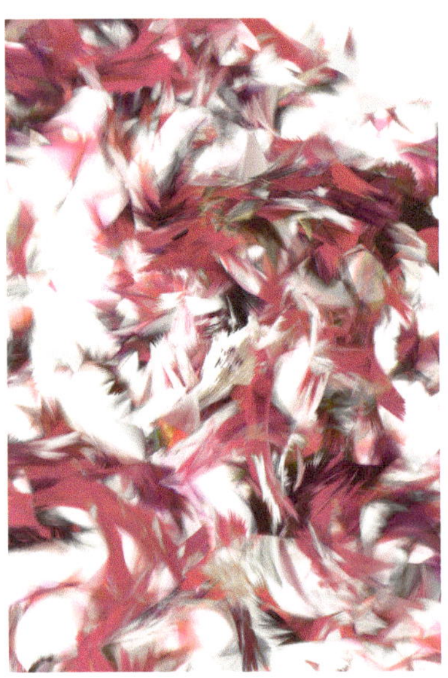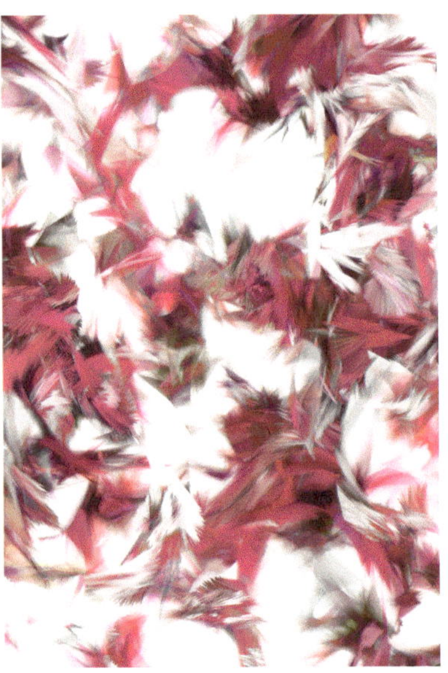

MOVEMENT. Casey Reas, **Process 18 (Image B 9, 10)**, 2010. Pair of
unique c prints, each 17.125 x 11.25 inches. © *Casey Reas. Courtesy of*
bitforms gallery, New York.

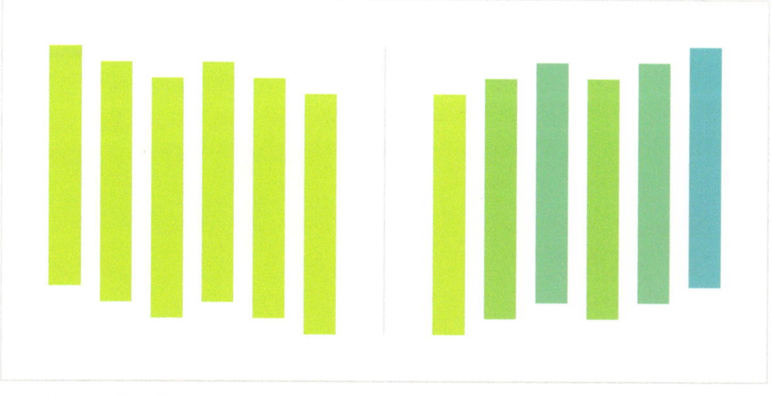

Figure 8-9

In addition to the illusion of space, color can also provide a sense of movement. One method to suggest movement in a composition is repetition. Repeated colors that are placed near one another suggest slow movement, while repeated colors that are spread out suggest a faster speed. A sense of movement can also be generated through a color progression or gradient. Gradual changes in color suggest slow movement, while rapid changes in color suggest faster movement. Color progressions can be combined with an illusion of depth to suggest movement through space, and not simply lateral movement across the surface of the picture plane (8-9).

Finally, the use of color significantly influences the overall unity of a composition. While contrast in color adds variety, color repetition or similarity promotes a sense of organization. The use of discernible color schemes enhances the unity of a composition. Simple color schemes with monochromatic, analogous, or complementary hue relationships provide a greater sense of unity than more complex double-comple-mentary, split-complementary, triad, or tetrad hue relationships. But the use of any defined hue relationship provides greater

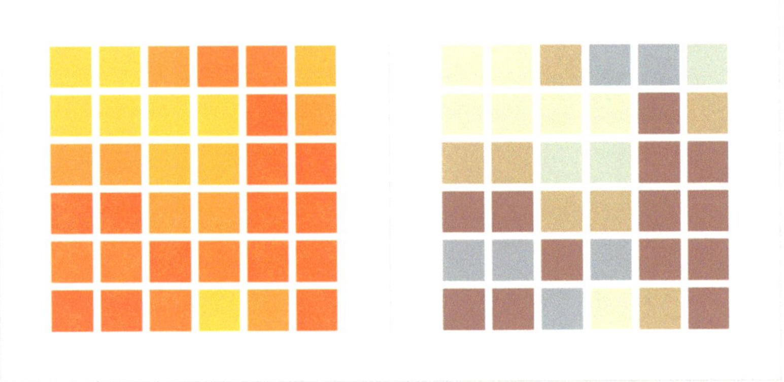

Figure 8-10

unity than a color scheme with unrelated hues. The overall use of value and saturation in a composition will additionally affect its unity. A consistent use of value such as a high-key, intermediate-key, or low-key color scheme, or a consistent use of saturation such as a chromatic, neutral, or achromatic color scheme will promote unity (8-10). Color schemes with too much variation in value or overly saturated colors can work against a sense of unity.

As we have seen throughout this text, color is a complex and powerful visual quality. There is no limit to its exploration. Color constantly surprises and inspires. It triggers strong emotions and memories. Artists and designers should dedicate themselves to the continuous study of color by consciously observing how color behaves in the world around them. In this way, we can begin to understand how colors are perceived and defined, how colors influence one another, and ultimately, how to utilize color effectively as a tool for communication and expression.

GLOSSARY

Achromatic

Achromatic colors are without saturation and have no discernible hue (26).

Additive

Color that is experienced directly, as projected light, is classified as additive color (32).

Aerial Perspective

Aerial perspective occurs when distant objects are viewed through a layer of atmosphere, causing them to appear blurry, cool in hue, uniform in value, and weak in saturation. Also known as Atmospheric Perspective (78).

Afterimage

An afterimage is an apparent image that is perceived after a visual stimulus is removed from our field of vision (63).

Analogous

When multiple hues neighbor each other on a color wheel, they are considered to be analogous (46).

Atmospheric Perspective

See Aerial Perspective (78).

Chroma

See Saturation (24).

Chromatic

Chromatic colors have a noticeable level of saturation, allowing their hue quality to be perceptible (25).

CMYK

CMYK is an abbreviation for cyan, magenta, yellow, and black, the colors used when printing with transparent ink (39).

Color

A color is defined by its unique combination of hue, value, and saturation (8).

Color Palette

See Color Scheme (44).

Color Progression

A color progression is a series of even visual steps between any two colors (57).

Color Scheme

A selection of colors used for a specific application is a color scheme. Also known as Color Palette (44).

Color Vibration

Color vibration describes a visual experience where the edges between adjacent colors appear to shimmer and vibrate (66).

Color Wheel

A color wheel is a basic tool that organizes the primary, secondary, and tertiary hues of a color system into a circle (33).

Complementary

Two hues that lie directly opposite one another on a color wheel are considered complementary (48).

Cool

Hues such as green and blue, which are associated with foliage, water, and snow, are considered cool (11).

Dissonance

Color dissonance suggests a conflicting combination of colors that is unbalanced and chaotic (44).

Double-Complementary

A double-complementary hue relationship utilizes two sets of complementary hues and is usually constructed from two adjacent hues on the color wheel combined with their corresponding complementary hues (50).

Fluting

Fluting arises in a sequence of successive color steps where the illusion of a gradient is created across the surface of each color (69).

Gamut

The gamut of a color system is the full range of colors that can be produced using its primary hues (41).

Gradient

A gradient is a progression in color with a continuous transition, eliminating any discrete steps between the parent colors (57).

Harmony

Color harmony suggests a pleasing combination of colors that is ordered and balanced (44).

High-Key

High-key values range from white to light gray on the value scale (53).

Hue

Hue is the name of a color in its purest state (8).

Intensity

See Saturation (24).

Intermediate-Key

Intermediate-key values sit between light gray and dark gray on the value scale (53).

Light

Light is a form of electromagnetic radiation that can be perceived by the human eye (3).

Low-Key

Low-key values range from dark gray to black on the value scale (54).

Monochromatic

A monochromatic color scheme employs a single, fixed hue (45).

Neutral

Neutral colors have a low level of saturation, making their hue quality less distinguishable (26).

Normal Value

The normal value of a hue is its inherent value when at maximum saturation (20).

Optical Mixing

Optical mixing occurs when small areas of color appear to blend visually to form a new color (65).

Primary

A hue is considered primary in a given color system if it cannot be obtained through the mixture of other hues (33).

Process Colors

Colors derived through a combination of cyan, magenta, yellow, and black inks are known as process colors (40).

RGB

RGB is an abbreviation for red, green, and blue, the primary hues of light (36).

ROYGBIV

The hues of the visible spectrum are commonly abbreviated as ROYGBIV for red, orange, yellow, green, blue, indigo, and violet (3).

RYB

RYB is an abbreviation for red, yellow, and blue, the primary hues of paint (34).

Saturation

Saturation is the relative strength or purity of a color. Also known as Intensity or Chroma (24).

Secondary

Mixing two primary hues of a color system in equal proportions creates a secondary hue (33).

Shade

A shade is a color variation generated by adding black to a hue (29).

Simultaneous Contrast

Simultaneous contrast describes the apparent shift in color that occurs between neighboring colors where their similarities are reduced and their differences are emphasized (63).

Split-Complementary

A split-complementary hue relationship is a variation of a complementary hue relationship that replaces the hue at one end of a complementary pair with two neighboring hues on the color wheel (49).

Subtractive

Color that is experienced indirectly, as reflected light, is classified as subtractive color (32).

Tertiary

Mixing a primary hue of a color system with an associated secondary hue creates a tertiary hue (33).

Tetrad

Four hues that are equidistant from one another on a color wheel have a tetrad relationship (52).

Tint

A tint is a color variation generated by adding white to a hue (29).

Tone

A tone is a color variation generated by adding gray to a hue (29).

Triad

Three hues that are equidistant from one another on a color wheel have a triad relationship (51).

Value

Value is the relative lightness or darkness of a color (16).

Value Scale

A value scale is a sequence of grays, from white to black, used to measure the value of an individual color (17).

Vanishing Boundaries

Vanishing boundaries describes a visual experience where the edges between adjacent colors become indistinct and difficult to discern (67).

Visible Spectrum

The wavelengths of light that can be perceived by the human eye form the visible spectrum, with individual wavelengths corresponding to distinct hues of color (3).

Warm

Hues such as red, orange, and yellow, which are associated with sunlight and fire, and considered warm (11).

CPSIA information can be obtained
at www.ICGtesting.com
Printed in the USA
LVHW07n1612010718
582421LV00007B/52/P